Careers in Media

Careers in Media

Second Edition

Michael P. Savoie

Valdosta State University

Frank Barnas

Valdosta State University

Allyn & Bacon

Boston   New York   San Francisco
Mexico City   Montreal   Toronto   London   Madrid   Munich   Paris
Hong Kong   Singapore   Tokyo   Cape Town   Sydney

Acquisitions Editor: Jeanne Zalesky
Series Editorial Assistant: Megan Lentz
Production Editor: Karen Walter
Editorial Production Service: Laserwords Maine
Manufacturing Buyer: JoAnne Sweeney
Electronic Composition: Laserwords India
Cover Administrator: Joel Gendron

10 9 8 7 6 5 4 3 2 1   13 12 11 10 09

Allyn & Bacon
is an imprint of

www.pearsonhighered.com

ISBN-10:   0-205-72381-0
ISBN-13: 978-0-205-72381-2

Contents

Acknowledgments

This book would not have been written without the support of the Mass Media Area, the Department of Communication Arts, the College of the Arts, and Valdosta State University. Additionally, VSU's Career Services provided information on databases, texts, and statistics referenced throughout the book, and the advisory columns in the Portfolio Development chapter stem from that office. On the editorial side, Taina Brezault served as the research assistant for the text, locating and developing data on websites, media outlets, and employment trends.

The authors are also indebted to the Valdosta State University alumni who contributed their biographical information. Chris Walsh, Jessica Donaldson, Kevin Blackston, Michael Gebora, Josh Cook, Mickey Goodwin, Kevin Allison, Kylie Mitchell, Emily Harp, Evans Wilson, Crystle Roberson, Adam Sumner, Kate Gelsthorpe, Jason Tyler, Thomas Nay, Lacy Adams Dixon, Shana Dean Young, Christi Chase, Samantha Harden, and Jade Bulecza. While they highlight the outcome of diligence and hard work, they illustrate that students need not graduate from a large university in a major media market to succeed in mass media.

As always, an acknowledgment is due to the authors' families for their support throughout the writing of this book. This is for them.

Careers in Media

1 Overview of Media Careers

Introduction

In the expanding field of media, there are many career opportunities for students in traditional and new media. Although it is a popular discipline across college and vocational technical campuses, students in this field often focus on career objectives that are ambiguous and poorly planned. As in any practically oriented discipline, many media curricula emphasize learning the skills and tools of the trade. In addition to the primary areas of media production, many programs fail to address lateral but critical areas of production support. For many students of mass media, the road to success in a media career is not always direct or readily apparent. Life skills and analytical deduction are important in many occupations and are essential in pursuing a career in media. Given this premise, finding a job in a specific media area should reflect the essential skills of the trade rather than a broad or unspecific notion.

The objective of this book is to address employment concerns in media and to point out often overlooked options for students seeking jobs in the media world. Traditional media is an area that has enormous appeal to students, but hiring tends to be highly selective and competitive. Most media curriculums focus on practical experiential learning for positions in the upper echelon of traditional media. Recently, institutions began offering courses in new media that focus on the needs and demands of the digital revolution. As the worlds of new and traditional media continue to converge and consolidate, adaptable skills in production techniques will be invaluable for today's graduates.

An assessment of individual aptitude and a clear idea of one's career goal are essential in planning for a career in media. Interest in a particular discipline is a good start but is not a conclusive or focused objective. For example, many college programs offer students an opportunity to step into a primary production role with little or no experience. After one or two prerequisite courses, students are capable of stepping into a role of management or coordination of a project. In contrast, the professional world is not as judicious. Qualifications, initiative, and aptitude often dictate placement and mobility in the world of media. In order to achieve one of these highly competitive positions, it is often necessary to begin in an entry-level position. It can be disheartening to "start at the bottom," but it is essential in establishing self-worth and credibility in any media environment.

In addition to a positive and enthusiastic attitude, a set of goals must be part of any successful plan. It is not realistic to plan to fulfill all career objectives with one goal. Any successful career will take years, and incremental moves are needed to achieve a life-fulfilling career in media. It is often presumptuous to bypass the prerequisite professional experience necessary to be competent and proficient in a given area of expertise. One reason for this preoccupation with proficiency is the cost involved with the production and dissemination of mass media. By its nature, communication to a mass audience is a costly endeavor. The larger the target audience, the more costly it is to produce. However, it is also more profitable. As part of serving the common good of society, mass media functions to inform, entertain, and advertise. Mass media, by its nature, are a means of profit. If this were not the case, mass media would cease to exist. Having a clear understanding of this premise is essential in planning for a career in media. Understanding the objective of a media organization is important in developing a strategy for success. According to the Department of Labor's *Occupational Outlook Handbook*, "Making informed career decisions requires reliable information about opportunities in the future."

In an exit survey, mass media students were asked to submit their career objectives after graduation. Some of the comments are as follows: "...I plan to work with music. Either with a record label, in a band, DJ or at a radio station." "...After graduation, I plan to work with video and film producers." "I might want to do something like directing or producing a news show." "I'm interested in working as a television news writer." "I would like to direct a sitcom or motion pictures." "...I plan on working in the field with Internet sports media." This sampling of career objectives is not reflective of the practical training provided as part of a media curriculum. These students' comments are statements of fulfillment but do not specify clear career objectives and incremental goals. They reflect the lack of knowledge of the job market and the lack of a prudent approach to securing a position in the world of professional media. In addition, many of the objectives refer to careers that are highly competitive and require years of on-the-job development and conditioning. A more realistic and often overlooked approach is to pursue entry-level positions with the notion that through hard work and perseverance, more desirable career positions are attainable.

In reference to the student survey, there is another glaring omission in successfully achieving career objectives. Many of the comments do not clearly articulate a specified occupation or career. Most are broad in scope and do not offer references to specific companies, geographic settings, or long-term considerations. In the first comment concerning working with music, the object is not only vague but it is not even consistent with a specific media area. The comment specifying interest in working as a television news writer is clear but does not offer enough specific information and fails to articulate the many levels and positions involved in securing a position in writing for television. The fundamental issue of poor planning and goal setting is often the first impediment in securing a position in media.

Quite often media students seek positions that are characterized with a dramatic rise to stardom. The appeal of movie stardom, national radio personalities, and respected journalists is considerable. But for every star or famous personality in front of the camera, there is a host of positions and support personnel working to create, disseminate, and promote specific media projects. As essential cogs in the machine, all positions related to the production of media are significant and necessary. Given the notion of mass media dissemination, the costs and organizational structure of any media endeavor are daunting and require careful coordination of teams of personnel. As a consequence, the media industry continues to grow and seek innovation and creative talent.

Occupational Statistics

According to the U.S. Bureau of Labor Statistics Office of Occupational Statistics and Employment Projections (2008–2009), "Occupations for which a bachelor's degree is the most significant source of education or training are expected to gain the largest share of employment over the 2006-2016 decade, rising from 12.3 percent in 2006 to 13.0 percent in 2016." Given this statistic, students pursuing bachelor's degrees will see increased opportunity in occupations over the next couple of years. The Bureau of Labor Statistics (BPL, 2008–2009) states, "Taking growth and replacement needs into consideration, a greater proportion of total job openings are projected to be filled by workers with at least some college rather than by those with a high-school degree or less. An estimated 57.3 percent of job openings are expected to be filled by those with some college or a bachelor's or higher degree, whereas 42.7 percent of jobs are expected to be filled by those with only a high school degree or less." In addition, there will be an increase in the area of self-employment. In reference to these employment increases, the chart below reinforces the notion that higher education correlates to greater earnings and lower unemployment.

In relation to careers in media, the Bureau of Labor Statistics categorizes media occupations in the area of professional and related occupations. Employment in this area is projected to be the fastest growing area of any group. This category will grow by 23.3 percent and add 4.1 million new jobs (BLS, 2008–2009). In the area of self-employment, most growth is projected in two subgroups: (1) arts, design, entertainment, sports, and media occupations and (2) computer occupations. It is projected that self-employment will add 305,000 new jobs, although 1 in 5 is expected to be held by self-employed workers. Most companies are inclined to purchase these workers' services rather than hiring them on a full-time basis. In addition, the demand for new media and computer-related occupations will continue to

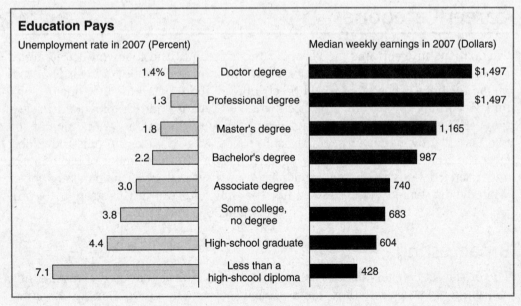

Education Pays

Unemployment rate in 2007 (Percent)		Median weekly earnings in 2007 (Dollars)
1.4%	Doctor degree	$1,497
1.3	Professional degree	$1,497
1.8	Master's degree	1,165
2.2	Bachelor's degree	987
3.0	Associate degree	740
3.8	Some college, no degree	683
4.4	High-school graduate	604
7.1	Less than a high-shcool diploma	428

Source: 2008–2009 Occupational Outlook Handbook Bureau of Labor Statistics, Current Population Survey.

increase as a result of advances in technology, media convergence, and Internet technologies related to media development. According to Department of Labor statistics (2008–2009), "Employment in the information super sector is expected to increase by 6.9 percent, adding 212,000 jobs by 2016. Information technology contains some of the fast-growing computer-related industries such as software publishing, Internet publishing and broadcasting, and wireless telecommunication carriers. Employment in these industries is expected to grow by 32 percent, 44.1 percent, and 40.9 percent, respectively. The information super sector also includes motion picture production; broadcasting; and newspaper, periodical, book, and directory publishing. Increased demand for telecommunications services, cable service, high-speed Internet connections, and software will fuel job growth among these industries" (BLS, 2008–2009).

The Bureau of Labor Statistics provides additional statistical data supporting employment growth. (The BLS tables are available on the Internet at www.bls.gov.) In the category of broadcasting, all occupations will have an increase of 9.4 percent between 2006 and 2016. In the category of Motion Picture and Video Industries, all occupations will have an increase of 10.9 percent between 2006 and 2016. In the category of Advertising and Public Relations, all occupations will have an increase of 13.6 percent between 2006 and 2016. In addition, media usage and consumer spending will increase to $880.87 per person per year over the next decade, according to *Veronis Suhler Stevenson Communications Industry Forecast* (2008), an annual publication on communications forecasts.

In light of the projected job opportunities and increasing media usage and consumer spending, media students will continue to see opportunities in media-related occupations. In regard to these projections, the concern is not the statistical data or availability of jobs but how to find employment. Any successful career objective must address employment that will be fulfilling and is suited to an individual's area of expertise and training.

Career Categories

Occupations in electronic media are categorized into the following three areas: (1) broadcasting, (2) motion picture and video industries, and (3) advertising and public relations. These topics will be covered in more detail in subsequent chapters. According to the Office of Occupational Statistics and Employment Projections (BLS, 2008–2009), "Professional and related occupations will be one of the two fastest growing major occupational groups, and will add the most new jobs. Over the 2006–2016 period, a 16.7 percent increase in the number of professional and related jobs is projected, which translates into nearly 5 million new jobs." While media-related industries are not the only category in this group, the projected growth is expected to continue between 2006 and 2016.

Broadcasting

The broadcast category consists of industries of networks that create, license, and distribute programs, whether they be television or radio production. As an industry, broadcasting is fast-paced and ever changing. Because the field is exciting, unique, and perceived as glamorous, positions in broadcasting are highly competitive. Often requiring a college degree in a related field, jobs in broadcasting require a certain level of professional proficiency. Although a college degree in a related

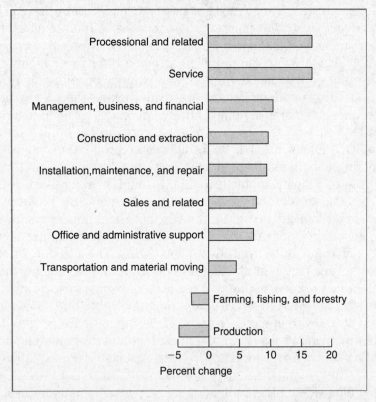

Source: Bureau of Labor Statistics for Professional and Related Occupations,
2008–2009.

broadcasting discipline is valued, relevant work experience is preferred in the world of professional broadcasting. With approximately 450 institutions offering degree programs in journalism and mass media disciplines, graduates of broadcast-related disciplines dominate competition in the broadcast field.

The two main areas in broadcasting consist of television and radio. Broadcasting is commonly referred to as traditional media but as Internet usage further erodes broadcast audiences, broadcasters are increasingly delivering their programming via the Internet. Although Internet delivery of broadcast media is on the rise, the number of program personnel and news staff is declining. Conversely, computer specialists in the broadcast category are expecting a 24.4 percent increase in employment opportunities. This is one of the largest increases in the media field, second only to sales representatives.

Television

Television networks broadcast a variety of programs locally and nationally. The television area can therefore be further segmented into local and national career opportunities. In the national arena, television networks encompass network news operations, produce entertainment programming, and provide programming to local network affiliates.

Network news operations are highly stratified, offering many employment opportunities for media students. With a similar structure to local news operations, an understanding of the practical application of media is highly valued in occupations in this area. Most employers prefer experience for these positions and usually require a degree in journalism or a related media field. Positions in national network news production are highly competitive and often require candidates to have local news experience. It is common for persons employed in these organizations to have experience in smaller markets to earn or prove their abilities in front of a much smaller audience. Candidates who have an extensive resume or body of work unquestionably demonstrate the proficiency required for these highly competitive positions. In addition to the in front of the camera positions of news analyst, reporters, and correspondents, there are many behind-the-scenes positions for technical production positions. Some of these opportunities include directors, producers, writers, editors, technical directors, computer graphics operators and designers, videographers, and a list of other related production occupations.

The working conditions in broadcast news are fast paced and often hectic. Employment in this highly sophisticated and complex area of broadcasting often requires frequent travel and relocation. Employment in broadcast news is expected to increase over the next ten years, but the numbers will be lower than the average growth in employment due to media consolidation, introduction of new technologies, and competition from other media outlets. The introduction of new technology is a relevant factor in slowing growth in this area, but positions in new media areas in news broadcasting will see above average growth in employment. Online news sites are widespread as many traditional news outlets adapt new technologies to keep up with audience trends. These changes are reflected in most of the major news organizations that provide content and programming on the Internet. According to a study conducted by the Associated Press (2008), "Today's youth receive their news from far more sources than older people, consuming media from online video, blogs, online social networks, mobile devices, RSS, word of mouth, Web portals and search engines."

Producing episodic and serial programming is another area of national television broadcasting. Although most television programs are produced by the motion picture industry, it is the responsibility of television broadcast personnel to oversee distribution, dissemination, and scheduling of these programs. As part of the entertainment area of television networks, producers and network representatives are often employed to coordinate projects produced for television. As with television news positions, these positions are highly competitive and require on-the-job experience beyond the scope of a post-secondary degree. Many of the people filling these positions have worked in the entertainment industry and have a proven track record or wealth of experience.

Local broadcast television offers many entry-level positions to graduates of media programs. With the greater concentration of jobs in larger cities or markets, entry-level positions are most often available in a smaller market or in less populated regions of the United States. In local broadcast television markets, the areas of employment include news, production, promotion, sales, and management.

Local news outlets are structured similarly to national network news operations. Quite often affiliated with a major network, local news outlets are the breeding grounds for up-and-coming talent. It is often possible to secure a position in small market news operation with little or no experience with a post-secondary degree in journalism or a related media discipline. Although expertise in production and proficient writing skills are expected, many of these positions offer on-the-job training. A typical entry-level position includes producers, reporters, and other behind-the-scenes support. The hours are usually long and the schedule is erratic. Working on holidays and weekends is part of the entry-level routine. In addition, entry-level personnel often are required to function in many different capacities and roles. Some of the fundamental premises of any position in media are the ability to adapt, be versatile, and to solve problems.

Aside from careers in news or journalism, local television stations offer opportunities for technical and creative-minded individuals. Many local broadcast stations have production and promotion departments that produce local commercials, community shows, and promotional spots. Occupations in television broadcasting require skills more conducive to film and narrative video programs or disciplines. Typical positions broadcasting include producers, directors, editors, writers, and computer graphics designers. Entry-level positions in television are wonderful opportunities to develop the necessary skills to secure lateral occupations in the world of motion picture production or corporate video production.

Radio

Careers in radio broadcasting are also segmented into local and national categories. One of the most volatile and rapidly changing areas of broadcasting, it is difficult to predict the trends that will dictate standards for jobs in radio. With consolidation, media convergence, and new technologies, careers in radio will see a slight decrease in job opportunities. Although on-air opportunities in radio will decline by 9.7 percent, the industry continues to offer viable entry-level occupations in media. An occupation in radio can provide experience that will translate to other areas of audio production. Job growth for motion-picture sound engineers is 18.3 percent and for broadcasting, is 6.2 percent.

As in television broadcasting, national network radio is highly stratified but offers entry-level and support positions to media graduates. Job experience, a proven track record and a post-secondary degree in a related discipline are often required or requisite on the local level. Recent changes in FCC regulations and radio consolidation have threatened or limited opportunities in local markets for entry-level positions. In recent years, larger media companies have purchased stations nationwide. In an attempt to reduce operating costs, consolidation of sales, production, and management have proven effective in saving money, but the results have produced limited employment growth. This trend has continued, and changes in FCC policy regarding media ownership have not been favorable in terms of job growth and opportunities. Other major threats to the radio industry include satellite and Internet radio, CD sales, and music downloading sites for personal media players like Apple's iPod.

The greatest impact on radio broadcasting has been the introduction of new technologies. As an industry that is in transition from traditional to new media, jobs in computer and technology-related areas will see an increase in job opportunities over the next ten years. Conventional occupations in broadcasting required a high degree of specialization to operate older equipment with a clearly defined role or knowledge of a specific area. Newer computerized equipment that is multifunctional, relatively easy to operate, and can be purchased at a lower cost is replacing outdated specialized equipment. This has greatly reduced specialized areas of expertise and the need for workers who were trained on this highly complicated equipment.

Motion Picture and Video Industries

The U.S. motion picture industry produces most of the world's popular entertainment. The venues for this entertainment include theatrically released feature films, episodic television series, sitcoms, music videos, and direct-to-video movies. These occupations, dominated by major studios and television networks, employ a variety of technical and creative personnel. In general, college programs prepare students for occupations in motion picture industries, but technical expertise and professional experience are highly valued and often preferred. As these positions are highly competitive, it is essential that a recent graduate of a mass media or film program exhibit adaptable and analytical skills that are hallmarks of the employees of the industry. Unlike other areas of employment, the motion picture and video industries rely on experienced and seasoned individuals to solve problems and support the production process. In contrast to other professional areas, a post secondary degree in a related field is not required nor does it assure employment in this category of occupations.

The world of professional motion picture and video production is perceived to be glamorous. In fact, it is arduous and tiring work. In spite of this, it is still an appealing and highly competitive work environment. A production company that hires personnel on a need basis, rather than employing full-time personnel coordinates most production. Freelance employment, as it is called in the industry, is standard operating procedure. Personnel are usually attached to a production until it is completed. In the case of a major feature film, this employment period can range from one to several months. In episodic television production, employment might last years. Another factor related to the term of employment is on-the-job performance and the ability to work long and difficult hours. Given the costs associated with motion picture and video production, the adage "time is money" is the mantra of every savvy producer.

In addition to on-the-job experience and proficiency, it is often essential for personnel to join a guild or union. As the motion picture and television industry is highly unionized, opportunities for non-union personnel are limited. As most professional production is done in Los Angeles and New York, a recent graduate of a mass media or film program would be well served by moving to one of these thriving centers. In addition to Los Angeles and New York, several other cities have created a small professional production niche. These cities include: Chicago, Illinois; Orlando, Florida; Irving, Texas; Wilmington, North Carolina; and New Orleans, Louisiana.

There are a variety of technical and creative positions employed in the motion picture and video industry. Technical positions include cinematographers, editors, sound engineers, computer specialists, and electricians. Creative positions include directors, producers, writers, and actors. There are many other areas that combine both the technical and creative or behind-the-scenes resources that are essential to any production. These careers include production designers, post-production audio editors and engineers, computer graphic designers, animators, and other related positions. Within these occupations, on the job training is preferred. Unfortunately for college graduates, this experience can take years to accumulate. Since these jobs are highly sophisticated and require years of on-the-job training and apprenticeship, they are not often filled by entry-level personnel such as recent college or technical school graduates. Positions that are considered entry level and accessible to ambitious graduates include menial support positions such as production assistants, office personnel, and interns. An intern position is a great opportunity, since success in the industry is about exposure and time on the job. Although it is humbling to start at the proverbial bottom of the production field, resourcefulness and a positive attitude do much to further a creative and focused individual. It would be naïve to think a student could walk into a production environment and secure a professional production position without experience. With many degree programs in mass media, video, and film production, the motion picture and video industries have an almost unlimited pool of potential employees. It is often an individual's perseverance, fortitude, and attitude that assure success in the industry.

According to the Bureau of Labor Statistics (2008–2009), "employment in the motion picture and video industries is projected to grow 10.9 percent between 2006 and 2016." The growth in the entertainment industry is attributed to the need for programming to fill the many channels available through diverse distribution outlets, such as satellite, cable, DVD, and the Internet. In addition to domestic markets, there is a tremendous demand for American productions abroad. These foreign markets, combined with domestic demand, offer many opportunities to graduates in the entertainment-related fields. As with the broadcasting category, new media and digital technologies will offer even greater opportunities to individuals. As computers and digital technologies transform the entertainment industry, these skills will be invaluable to the industry and prospective employees. Given the transformation from traditional to new media technologies, students currently training for positions in the motion picture and video industries should take advantage of courses that prepare them in these areas. In addition to the time and money spent on training for these occupations, it is imperative that students interested in this field utilize the expertise and equipment provided by college and university media programs.

Advertising and Public Relations

Advertising and public relations agencies develop and prepare advertisements for companies and organizations to promote their interests and image. This industry employs a variety of experts related to the development of these campaigns and the dissemination of their message. Advertising and public relations companies utilize all forms of media including print, radio, television, and the Internet. According to the Bureau of Labor Statistics, "there are about 48,000 advertising and public relations services establishments in the United States." Many of these agencies focus on one medium or specific group to represent. Some companies in this category function solely as media brokers, buying and reselling advertising time or space. Therefore, companies in this category employ a variety of creative and business-minded personnel. One agency may employ writers, graphic artists, and other media production personnel, while other agencies may employ print, radio, and television buyers.

The objective of these firms is to sway or persuade opinion regarding a product, opinion, group, or political position. Public relations firms specifically help secure favorable public exposure for their clients and help them deal with any relevant media situation. This includes dissemination of product information, public awareness, or political agenda. The lobbying firm is a particular type of public relations firm that works through government and legislatures to further a particular issue, industry, or organization to attain a certain public image.

Most advertising and public relations agencies are small and competition for employment in this industry is highly competitive. According to the Bureau of Labor Statistics (2008–2009), "California and New York together account for about 1 in 5 firms and more than 1 in 4 workers in the industry." Given this statistic, it is advantageous to relocate to one of these major metropolitan areas to further or develop a career in advertising or public relations. Positions in this category include account managers, creative directors, media directors, public relations specialists, copywriters, art directors, graphic designers, market researchers, media planners, and buyers. Although there are many other positions in advertising and public relations, agencies specializing in specific areas will employ related or specifically needed occupations. It is common for advertising and public relations positions to require a post-secondary degree. Employers prefer candidates to have related degrees in journalism, English, communications, business, or more recently a specific concentration in public relations.

The advertising and public relations industry is expected to grow by 13.6 percent between 2006 and 2016. With job growth slightly above average for all industries, the increase is due to the expanding economy with more products and services to advertise. In addition to this expansion, new technologies will streamline the use of media and means of dissemination. As with other related media categories, new media skills will play an important role preparing for the advertising and public relations field.

Conclusion

As most media-related careers will see an increase over the next ten years, the outlook for new graduates of media programs is optimistic, although this optimism should not be mistaken as a guarantee or assurance of a job after graduation. The recurring theme present in all forecasts for occupations in media is the need for skills in new media and digital technologies. Computer-related occupations will see the greatest growth in all areas of media. In assessing career objectives, students should contemplate these objectives before completing any curriculum in mass media, journalism, communications, or film. Many schools tend to focus on traditional forms of media. In recent years, media programs have begun to incorporate new media and computer skills as part of their curriculum. Although these skills are important and relevant, they are not necessarily the only skills needed for success. Training in media must orient students to be creative, analytical, and adaptive thinkers. These skills are necessary for any successful career in media. The ability to solve problems and adapt are fundamental and essential. As most graduates will begin in entry-level or subordinate support roles, the only assurance of success is based on a positive attitude, hard work, and dedication.

Throughout this book, the areas outlined in this chapter will be dissected and analyzed to offer a realistic perspective in pursuing a career in media. Biographies are dispersed in each chapter to offer first-person testimonials of day-to-day routines and requirements of entry-level occupations. As stated earlier, many failures are realized when the job does not live up to an individual's expectation. In forming a career objective, careful consideration must be given to the path that must be taken to fulfill a career objective. In particular, the transition from traditional media to new media consumption provides students with invaluable career guidance. In a recent class on an introduction to electronic media, students were asked two questions, "What media do you consume?" and "What are your occupational goals?" The majority of the class specified career goals in traditional media occupations, but then stated that their media consumption was exclusively new media such as the Internet and wireless technologies. This reinforces the notion that many students beginning their media education are preoccupied with the practical application of media but lack an understanding of the trends in media. Lucid and thoughtful consideration must be given to a career choice, as well as an understanding of the trends outlined in occupational projections. One of the shortcomings of post-secondary education is the failure to realize this premise. Training is not the same as planning for a career. Although the training is expected and relevant, planning and realistic goals are essential.

R-E-F-E-R-E-N-C-E-S

Career Guide to Industries 2008–2009. U.S. Bureau of Labor Statistics. U.S. Department of Labor, 2008. www.bls.gov.

Household Data Annual Averages. Department of Labor, Bureau of Labor Statistics, 0000

A New Model for News: Studying the Deep Structure of Young-Adult News Consumption. The Associated Press and the Context-Based Research Group, June 2008.

Occupational Outlook Handbook 2008–2009. U.S. Bureau of Labor Statistics. U.S. Department of Labor, 2008. www.bls.gov.

Siegelbaum, D. J. "A Bite-Sized Media Future." 3 June 2008 <http://www.time .com>

Statistical Abstract of the United States: 2008, 127th Edition. (Washington, D.C.: U.S. Census Bureau, 2007).

VSS Communications Industry Forecast, Annual. (New York, NY. 2007).

2 Print, Magazine, and Photojournalism

The Written Word

Employment in print media may be broadly divided into two areas: (1) editorial, which provides content, and (2) non-editorial, which is the business side of getting the actual newspaper or magazine printed and distributed. Many journalism school graduates target the writing and editorial careers, although opportunities in marketing, circulation, and production should not be overlooked.

Further divisions occur in print media in the physical classification of periodicals, which may be newspapers or magazines. Newspapers are overwhelmingly local, daily products that concern a specific regional audience. Magazines span titles of international to local interest and can be segmented into two broad categories: (1) general interest magazines, which include familiar titles such as *People* and *TV Guide,* and (2) those that target more specific audiences, like *American Hunter* and *Tampa Bay Illustrated.*

Unlike other employment positions available throughout media, those in the editorial field in print concentrate on writing ability. While newer technologies may force the rethinking of employable skills in the visual and aural areas, the overriding concern of those entering the print media is the ability to write well under deadline pressure. The modes of physically printing and delivering the final product of a newspaper or a magazine may change, but the standard precursor to employment is the written word.

Before computer-assisted layout, stories were printed onto galley paper according to the typeface and font desired, trimmed of excess paper from around the edges, and pasted onto a template over a light table (a table with a backlit surface). Stories were then lined up and physically moved around, set in place on the template with hot wax or glue on the back of the pages. Once the stories were set in the desired arrangement, the finished pages were transferred to a printing plant, where the pages were printed.

With the advent of word processors and mobile Internet access, reporters now create and submit stories from virtually anywhere. Copy editors revise the submissions on the computer, unlike previous rewrites, which occurred with handwritten changes or on typewriters. Layout artists digitally construct the final product, moving stories, articles, headlines, and captions with the click of a mouse. Nevertheless, even with the technological advances that affect writing, editing, and layout, the skill level of the individual writers, editors, and layout artists is based upon the ability to write well under deadline pressure.

To summarize the positions available at newspapers and magazines, it is best to visualize the production process. Much like a television newsroom, an editor assigns a story to a reporter. The reporter researches, interviews, and gathers information. After writing the story, the reporter submits it to an editor, who checks the story for factual and stylistic errors. The layout artist then places the story into the newspaper or magazine layout, where pictures or illustrations are inserted. The last step is to add headlines and captions. The pages are proofread, and the final product is sent to press. The process may occur on a daily basis, as with most newspapers, or it may extend over a longer timeframe, such as for a weekly or monthly magazine.

Not all reporters give only a day to a certain story. Most reporters work on several stories simultaneously, with some having a tighter deadline than others. Some stories have deadlines spanning several weeks, especially if the piece is part of an ongoing news story, seasonal in nature, or a segment in an extended series of stories along a general theme.

Employment at magazines differs from jobs at newspapers, as magazines have more specific topics for their individual reading audiences. Writers at *Popular Mechanics*, for example, must use a different tone than those at *Time, Maxim*, or *Ladies' Home Journal*.

Newspapers

The major purpose of newspapers is to inform the public with detailed, timely, and objective coverage of the news, as well as to influence readers with editorials and advertising. The primary difference between newspapers and magazines is perspective. Though they may cover the same things, newspapers have immediate deadlines, while magazines have more time to develop a sense of perspective (Zimmerman, 1981).

One method of evaluating newspapers is to track their net revenue. The nation's top money-making newspaper is *USA Today*. Other newspapers that lead in revenue are located in large media markets, like the *Los Angeles Times*, *The New York Times*, and *The Miami Herald*.

Another way to rank newspapers is not by revenue, but by average daily circulation. *USA Today* and *The Wall Street Journal* are the nation's most-read newspapers, each selling more than two million copies a day. *The New York Times* ranks third in circulation, selling more than 1,100,000 daily, while the *Los Angeles Times* and *The Washington Post* round out the top five.

Magazines

Even with the development of new technologies for distributing information, printed magazines continue to thrive. The Magazine Publishers of America (MPA) reports 19,532 magazines were in circulation in 2007, 6,809 of which targeted consumers (MPA, 2008). The average reader spends 45 minutes reading each issue, and the MPA cites research from MediaVest that says that despite the abundance of online content, few consumers see the Internet replacing the print version of magazines in the next five years. Even so, the number of consumer magazine websites has increased 53 percent since 2004, and most magazines now have dedicated websites.

Personal Profile: *Chris Walsh*

Name, job title, place of employment, and city/state

Chris Walsh, Sports Writer, *Virgin Islands Daily News,* St. Thomas, US Virgin Islands

Job duties

I cover all of the local high school and college sporting events for the daily newspaper. I also cover national sailing and surfing events, as well as covering the Virgin Islands Olympic team. I write the stories and take photos for the paper and website.

What is a typical day like?

A typical day is going into the office and planning on the events to be covered. I will make a few phone calls to coaches or athletes then go to the event. After covering whatever event I attended, I go back to the office, write the story for tomorrow's paper, upload the story and photo for the website, then call it a night. Oh, my days usually start before work surfing in the beautiful blue ocean.

How did you obtain your job?

I had worked as a sports writer for three years for the *Valdosta Daily Times* and was able to couple that with my degree and experience from Valdosta State University to find the job. Before taking the job in the Virgin Islands I had applied to over 200 newspapers and television stations.

Job tips, hints, advice, or anecdotes

One job search tip would be to apply, apply, apply. Check the Internet everyday and make sure the job sites you are using are legitimate, with legitimate jobs. Even with experience coming out of college it took me 3 months to land a good job. Also, be ready to travel the country on interviews, so have some money put aside.

Salary

I make roughly $40,000 plus a year.

Advertising Age ranks magazines by two different measures: (1) ad pages (how many pages of the magazine are sold to advertisers) and (2) gross revenue. In 2005, the top magazines by ad pages were *People, The New York Times Magazine, InStyle, Forbes,* and *Fortune.* Only one of those magazines, *People,* also ranks near the top in gross revenue. In gross revenue rankings, the top five are *People, Sports Illustrated, Time, TV Guide,* and *Better Homes & Gardens.*

It is notable that these rankings are not based on paid subscriptions. In this category, other magazines, such as *Parade's* 32.5 million, or the 10 million who subscribe to *Reader's Digest,* dwarf *People's* 3.6 million subscribers.

Editorial Employment Sectors in Print

The editorial staff is comprised of editors, writers, designers, and photographers, all of whom create content. Generating story ideas, writing articles, and photo shoots fall under this broad category. The position of reporter/writer most often comes to mind, as a reporter interacts with the community on a daily basis.

Personal Profile: *Jessica Donaldson*

Name, title, and place of employment, and city/state?

Publisher of the *Glass Onion Newspaper,* Valdosta, Georgia. The Glass Onion is an independent newspaper promoting local music and entertainment.

Job duties

I oversee all content within the paper, including preparing the layout/graphic design as well as advertisement sales for the newspaper.

What is a typical day like?

Each day is unique, which is what makes my job great. One day I may be out on sales calls and the next I may be interviewing a band or working on graphic design for the new issue.

How did you obtain your job?

My first year after graduation I worked for a local radio group, which allowed me to network, and I made countless contacts. I was offered a job working for another independent newspaper and took the position. After two years of working for the company I realized that I could start my own newspaper, so I struck out on my own.

Search tips, hints, advice, or anecdotes?

Don't be hesitant to move for a job. If there isn't anything available in your field go where the jobs are. Also, don't take the first job that comes along. Make sure that

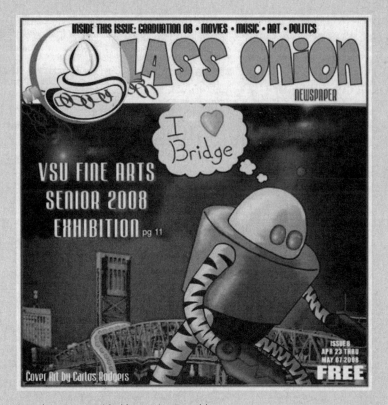

Sample cover provided by Jessica Donaldson

(continued)

Personal Profile: *Jessica Donaldson (continued)*

the position fits your personality. More importantly don't expect to strike it rich after college. It takes a great deal of time and experience to get where you are going. Be patient. It sounds cliché or redundant but do something that you love. Loving what you do is most important in the long run.

Salary

I am still in the first year of owning my own business so as of now I'm not at my salary goal, but I am working hard to build up advertisement. At the end of this year my salary is expected to be roughly $20,000 (which I can surprisingly live on).

The assignments fulfilled by reporters can vary dramatically. Thus, they are often delineated into the following categories:

BEAT REPORTER—Unlike television reporters, there is a greater opportunity to become a beat reporter in print, as most newspapers and magazines have specialized sections for areas such as politics, real estate, and business. Reporters in this area concentrate on their specific beats but may be called upon to cover breaking news as well.

GENERAL ASSIGNMENT REPORTER—This reporter handles assignments as they arise, often with no preset schedule during a given day. A general assignment reporter frequently covers accidents, crime, and press conferences. In this way, the reporter serves as the eyes and ears of the reading public with respect to daily breaking news. This position is found primarily at newspapers.

INVESTIGATIVE REPORTER—Much of the work performed by investigative reporters is secretive in nature, with the focus often on politicians or businesses. Those in this position are generally older and have reported for years, if not decades, as general assignment or beat reporters. This position is limited to newspapers in major markets or specialty magazines.

LIFESTYLE / FEATURE REPORTER—For some reporters, being a feature writer is the preferred outlet for their work, as they focus on items that do not fit the category of hard news. Personality profiles, consumer affairs, fashion, food, and similar topics are the domain of a lifestyle/feature reporter. Many magazines thrive in this category.

SPORTS REPORTER—Writing about sports is enticing, but it has evolved into a highly disciplined craft. Sports reporters at newspapers must cover national, state, and local sports, including college and high-school activities. Since so many sports events occur on weekends, the busiest time for sports reporters is when the news reporters have gone home.

The Editorial Staff

COPY EDITOR—Once the copy is written, it is submitted to a copy editor, who checks for factual errors, grammar, style, and usage. Each publication has multiple copy editors, some of whom specialize in certain fields, such as political or business news. The copy editor is also in charge of writing headlines for the stories, although some will accept suggestions from the reporters. Copy editors may have aides called proofreaders or editorial assistants.

EDITOR—Also called the editor-in-chief, this person sets policy and is the ultimate authority on the written content. Other editorial positions include news editors, managing editors, associate editors, and assistant editors, while some publishers also have sports editors, business editors, and other titles for those in charge of specific areas of the publication.

EDITORIAL WRITER—Not to be confused with an objective reporter, an editorialist offers a point of view in an editorial or opinion column in a newspaper. Editorial writers tend to be editors, although some senior level writers may also write opinion columns. Those who write opinions for their publication are essentially offering their point of view for public rebuttal. Editorial writers must be prepared to hear dissenting opinions from the community.

Related Editorial Positions

LAYOUT AND PAGE DESIGNER—As newspapers and magazines have evolved into computer-based publications, layout artists and page designers have incorporated more pictures, graphs, and visual aids for the reading audience. Unlike reporters and editors, who limit their output to word processing, layout artists use specific software and graphic interfaces to present their final publications.

PHOTOJOURNALIST—While technology has aided writers, copy editors, and layout designers, new digital cameras are a tremendous benefit for photojournalists. Many photojournalists float among the writers, working with the general assignment reporter for part of the day, later shooting a home's interior for a lifestyle reporter, and then taking photos of an evening sports event. While some photojournalists still rely on film cameras and subsequent film processing, more are turning to digital cameras since they can cover more events in the field and spend less time in the darkroom.

Non-Editorial Employment Sectors in Print

As specific positions and job titles at magazines vary according to the size, scope, and audience of the given title, this section addresses the categories of employment opportunities available at most publications.

ADMINISTRATION—The publisher, who heads the business department, is responsible for the overall operation and profitability of the magazine. Depending on the size of the magazine, the publisher may be assisted by an associate publisher, a chief financial officer, a general manager, and a number of assistants.

ADVERTISING AND SALES—Employees in advertising and sales are responsible for selling ad pages for each magazine issue, thereby generating income for the magazine. As with sales jobs in other areas of the media, a typical workday includes researching prospective leads and meeting with clients.

MARKETING—This sector can be divided into two units as defined by the target audience. One group is consumer marketers, who manage sales via subscriptions and single-copies, such as those bought at stores. The second marketing group designs media kits and plans events that promote the magazine. Additionally, they produce materials that can be used on sales calls or in presentations.

PRODUCTION—This group is responsible for physically producing the magazine, including placing advertising and editorial materials in the proper format, getting the materials to the printer, and distributing the magazine. It also oversees "breaking the book," or determining the number of editorial and advertising pages in each issue.

RESEARCH—The research department uses surveys, focus groups, and other tools to learn more about the magazine's readers and how to utilize the magazines' content. It then passes this information along to other areas to help shape editorial content and focus, thus maintaining solid sales and circulation.

Conclusion

According to the Bureau of Labor Statistics, employment of writers and editors is expected to grow about as fast as the average for all occupations through the year 2016, which is a 7 to 13 percent increase for the industry. The outlook for most writing and editing jobs is expected to be competitive, however, because many people with writing or journalism training are attracted to the occupation. As with other media careers, technological advances and consolidated media ownership will impact employment possibilities, but those with strong writing or editing skills should still be able to find desirable positions. The BLS notes that the median annual earnings for salaried writers and authors was $48,640 in May 2006, with earnings higher in advertising and related services than in newspaper, periodical, book, and directory publishers.

REFERENCES

"Building a Career in Magazines." *Magazine Publishers of America*. 28 Nov. 2005 <www.magazine.org/content/files/CareerInMags.pdf>.

Ferguson, Donald L., and Jim Patten. *Opportunities in Journalism Careers*. VGM Career Books, 2001.

Fischer, David. *The 50 Coolest Jobs in Sports*. ARCO Thomson Learning, 2001.

Goldberg, Jan. *Careers in Journalism*. Third edition. McGraw-Hill, 2002.

Magazine Publishers of America. 21 June 2008 <www.magazine.org/content/files/MPAHandbook0809.pdf>

Mogel, Leonard. *Careers in Communications and Entertainment*. Simon and Schuster, 2000.

U.S. Bureau of Labor Statistics. 21 June 2008 <www.bls.gov/oco/ocos089.htm>

Zimmerman, Caroline A. *How to Break into the Media Professions*. Doubleday, 1981.

3 Audio and Radio

The Evolution of Radio

In past years, working in radio was a natural precursor to working in television. While many talented on-air personalities stayed in radio positions, others honed their speaking and timing skills before venturing into television. But the training track has evolved. While there are complementary skills between the two media, many radio personalities remain in that realm, and television personalities do not see the need to work in radio before "advancing" to television.

Although radio predates television, its significance has declined in recent decades. For music, a media-savvy generation has been downloading songs, burning personalized compact discs, and compiling playlists on home computers. For news and sports, television and the Internet offer nonstop information. Even cell phone providers have impacted radio; users can subscribe to sports and news updates on their phones, making radio even more irrelevant. Simply put, radio doesn't enjoy the same impact as it did in years past.

The lack of influence and listeners, as stated above, can be traced to technology. First, the increased availability of portable music devices, exemplified by iPods and cell phones that hold music libraries, has affected how many listeners seek radio stations. Portable digital music consoles can hold thousands of songs in a device the size of a deck of cards. In addition, the next wave of broadcasting, known as podcasting, allows users to listen to live streams of music, sports, and news, thus effectively bypassing traditional radio waves.

According to Arbitron, a prominent media research firm that focuses primarily on the medium of radio, the weekly online radio audience increased to 33 million in 2008. On a weekly basis, online radio reaches 15 percent of 25- to 54-year olds. Additionally, the Internet is gaining on radio as the source people use to learn about new music. Arbitron notes "In 2008, radio is mentioned as the medium 'you turn to first to learn about new music' by about half of consumers (49 percent), with Internet at 25 percent. In 2002, radio was mentioned by nearly two-thirds of consumers (63 percent) for this perception, while only nine percent mentioned Internet."

Another trend impacting local radio is the creation of satellite radio provider Sirius XM Radio, which resulted from a merger of the Sirius and XM satellite radio companies. At its inception in July of 2008, Sirius XM Radio reached more than 18.5 million subscribers with more than 300 channels of programming. This makes it the second largest radio company, based upon revenue, in the country.

While Sirius XM employs programmers, air talent, and various other radio positions, the total number of employees is a fraction of what it would take to operate

300 comparable traditional radio stations. The advantage for listeners is the ability to enjoy a preferred format without the threat of ever losing the signal.

The disadvantage for radio employees is the loss of potential jobs. Additionally, what jobs do remain are often subject to consolidated ownership of "regular" radio stations. There are more than 13,000 radio stations in the United States and 3,800 station owners. Clear Channel Communications owns more radio stations than any other conglomerate, controlling about 1,200 of those stations. That is roughly 9 percent of U.S. radio stations and represents about 18 percent of the industry's revenue. Other leading radio conglomerates are CBS, Citadel Broadcasting, and Sirius/XM.

Arbitron reports that network radio reaches a nearly equal percentage of adult men (73 percent) and women (72 percent) on a weekly basis. Further, the audience age composition is well distributed, allowing radio stations to target their formats toward specific demographics, such as the middle aged or senior citizens.

Combining these factors provides an immediate employment correlation, with fewer positions available for job seekers at traditional radio stations. Between now and the year 2016, the Bureau of Labor Statistics forecasts the employment outlook for announcers to drop by 9.7 percent.

The Traditional Radio Industry

All radio stations need management, sales personnel, engineers, and announcers. The number of employees drops if a station is automated or is part of a group of stations in a market, but even then, personnel are needed to sell commercials, record advertisements, and keep the station on the air.

To work in radio, employees must not only be flexible with where the job is located geographically, but must also be accommodating in the format. The most popular format in the United States is Country music, thus there are more opportunities for new employees to work in that genre. The News/Talk format ranks next in popularity with Adult Contemporary a distant third. College students who want to work in an Urban Contemporary format will need to search for an opening; the number of Urban Contemporary stations is barely a tenth of those that play Country music.

Another consideration is the Average Quarterly Hour (AQH). The higher the AQH, the more listeners a format has, as the AQH counts how many listeners tune into a given station during a 15-minute span. Country is a strong format with both a large number of stations and a strong AQH share. Urban Contemporary has an AQH of 3.7, yet is only played by 154 stations—this depicts a profitable format on a small number of stations. Conversely, 724 stations play Contemporary Christian, yet its AQH is only 2.2. This shows many stations with fewer listeners.

These 15 popular formats only scratch the surface; Arbitron rates 54 formats in all. Other formats with fewer stations and smaller listening audiences include Jazz (0.4 AQH, 75 stations), Easy Listening (0.2 AQH, 46 stations), and Spanish Oldies (0.1 AQH, 26 stations).

For those who want to work in radio, it's vital to look beyond radio stations that play only the music that matches personal tastes. Most veteran radio personnel have, at one time or another, worked with a format that wasn't their first choice. Those who want to work in Country will find more opportunities than others, but those with a Jazz interest will find their options much more limited.

Employment Opportunities in Radio

There are radio job opportunities in three broad categories: (1) on-air and production, (2) news, and (3) sales and support. All categories answer to a general manager, who is responsible for the overall operation of a station. GMs have a solid knowledge of business and some technical understanding of how a station operates.

On-Air and Production

The best on-air personalities have knowledge of their music format, an easy rapport on the microphone, and a perfected sense of timing. In addition to their regular "on-air" duties, announcers also work with the production manager to voice local advertisements. Salaries for announcers tend to be low, with substantial paychecks available only in the larger markets.

ANNOUNCER—Also called disc jockeys (or DJs), they read news items and other information, such as community announcements and commercials breaks. They may take requests from listeners and frequently participate in "live remotes," which promote the station at community events. Those who host music shows must have a keen understanding of the music and performers. Announcers hosting news, talk, or sports programs must have a thorough knowledge of current events and be able to engage in conversations for long periods. Announcers are a radio station's "voice" and are often the people with whom the public identifies.

COPY WRITER—This staff member writes commercial and promotional copy in support of the station's sales, marketing, and promotion efforts. Announcers or members of the production crew often absorb many of the duties; thus, this position is not as commonly found as in years past.

PROGRAM DIRECTOR—This person not only directs the announcers, but is also responsible for a station's overall "sound," The program director schedules broadcasts, works with announcers, and is in charge of reaching the listening audience targeted by the station and its advertisers. He or she usually handles paperwork relating to budget, personnel, scheduling, and licensing.

PROMOTION DIRECTOR—This person promotes the station's image, programs, and activities through campaigns, remote music events, and on-air promotions. The promotion director also works with the sales department to develop and maintain a base of advertisers.

MUSIC DIRECTOR—This person is responsible for selecting music, managing the station's music library, and overseeing the daily music rotation. The music director relies on music popularity charts, sales records, demographic research, and listener requests to compile a list of music to be played. At some stations, this job is assumed by a senior disc jockey, while other stations now rely on satellite-fed music of a specific format.

PRODUCTION MANAGER—This person coordinates the creative output of the on-air personalities, including the recording and production of radio advertisements and public service announcements. They arrange recording sessions, oversee the production studios, and assign announcers to "voice" commercials. This person usually acts as the first line of defense for troubleshooting minor production problems (with more major concerns being addressed by the engineering department). At many stations, the production manager's duties are assumed by the program director.

News

True news positions are becoming harder to find in many markets, except at those stations dedicated to news and talk formats. Most news employees have broadcast journalism backgrounds and spend much of their time performing behind-the-scenes duties, such as interviewing, researching, and writing. Unless they host a long-format news program at a news station, only a fraction of their time is spent behind a microphone.

Personal Profile: *Kevin Blackston*

Name, job title, place of employment, and city/state

Kevin Blackston, Producer, WOKV-AM (Cox Radio), Jacksonville, Florida

Job duties

Write copy, edit audio, and voice wraps for morning news program.

What is a typical day like?

My shift starts at 10 p.m. For several hours I have the place to myself, writing stories for the morning news show. I chop up audio and scan the Internet for potential story ideas (such as national stories that can be localized). If there's a late-night murder or other incident, I get in touch with the police to get information. In addition, if there's "breaking news" such as a bad accident that's going to tie up traffic, I'll conduct phone interviews and write stories on that. My "day" officially ends at 6 a.m.

How did you obtain your job?

I sent out resumes and demo CDs. Then I sent out some more resumes and demo CDs, and my present employer contacted me and asked me to drive down for a visit. I actually interviewed for a reporter position, but was offered the producer spot. In terms of market size, it was a huge step up from my first radio job out of college, so I accepted.

Search tips, hints, advice, or anecdotes?

First, if there are particular stations or markets where you'd like to work, don't be afraid to send some samples even if there are no openings posted. I didn't know WOKV had any openings when I mailed my resume, but I ended up with a job. Besides, there tends to be a bit of turnover in this business, and your demo CD may still be sitting on the news director's desk when someone quits a couple of months down the road. Second, apply for jobs even if you don't have quite as much experience as a posting indicates you need. Obviously, if a company is looking for someone with five years of anchoring experience in a top 10 market, there's no need to apply for that job right out of college. On the other hand, if a job posting says you need at least a year of "real world" experience and you've been working part time for six months, send in a resume and some writing samples. A program director may see something he or she likes in what limited work you've done. Third, you probably won't get your dream job right off the bat. If you're offered a different position that lets you get your foot in the door, at least give it some consideration. Once you've proven you can do the "grunt work," there are more opportunities for

Personal Profile: *Kevin Blackston (continued)*

advancement. Finally, keep up with the news and do your research. Know the name of the U.S. secretary of state; know where thousands of people died last week due to an earthquake; know which third world country is currently in turmoil due to disputed elections. In addition, if you get an interview in a particular city, take time before that interview to find out who the mayor is. Which company is the city's biggest employer? Track down Web sites for the market's newspapers and TV stations, and scan the stories for the past couple of weeks to see what issues are making the headlines right now.

Salary

Less than $20,000/year. This is a job you do because you enjoy it, not because you plan to get rich. Keep in mind there may be benefits such as health insurance that aren't included in the salary you're offered. Ask questions to find out exactly what you'll get.

Radio news salaries, like those in television newsrooms, vary according to market size. According to Bob Papper of the Center for Media Design at Ball State University, the average radio news director salary is $36,400, but salaries range from a mere $9,000 to a high of $100,000. Other average salaries in radio stations span the sports reporter's $21,200 to the news anchor's $35,000. The maximum for news anchors, however, can range as high as $150,000.

NEWS DIRECTOR—As in television, the news director is the ultimate authority for what stories are covered. In addition to establishing the station's news policy, the news director supervises producers and reporters, monitors wire services, and sometimes serves as an on-air news presence. Since many music stations are curtailing their news departments and using satellite-fed national news updates, this position is usually available only in larger markets.

NEWS PRODUCER—A producer covers local news, writes news copy, and reads it on-air, essentially performing the combined duties of announcer, reporter, and producer. They monitor police scanners, localize national stories, and create entire newscasts. They may also cover traffic and weather-related news, as well as sports. Some stations in large markets still have news reporters who create individual stories, but most positions now require producers able to develop entire newscasts.

SPORTS DIRECTOR—This position is similar to the news director position, in that the sports director oversees the coverage of sports events on a local level. At community athletic events, the sports directors may perform live on-air duties, such as play-by-play coverage of the events. One entry-level position in sports radio is a color commentator, who is used during sports coverage to complement the play-by-play talent.

Sales and Support

Sales and management personnel do not necessarily come from media or communications backgrounds. Like any business, a background in accounting, business, or management can suffice for covering payroll, sales, and most managerial tasks. It is vital, however, to understand ratings and shares, which determines how much the

Personal Profile: *Michael Gebora*

Name, title, place of employment, and city/state?

Mike Gebora, Account Executive, Black Crow Media, Valdosta, Georgia

Job duties

I maintain consistent sales objectives by selling to key accounts and their agencies. I also obtain NTR or Non-Traditional Revenue through the development and execution of station promotions, contests, and events. Internet Revenue has become a major focus over the past 2-3 years.

What is a typical day like?

A typical day for an Account Executive is that nothing is typical; no two days are the same. You have to wear several hats throughout the day … from Sales Calls where you present (AND CLOSE) marketing campaigns to potential and existing clients, to writing copy or scripts and finally service and/or collection calls.

How did you obtain your job?

My start in Radio was as an Air Personality or DJ. After a couple of years of on-air work I was able to make the transition over to Sales. I believe that I have a competitive advantage over most Account Executives because I know and understand how promotions/contests are executed on air. I showed them my Mass Media degree from VSU.

Job search tips, hints, advice, or anecdotes?

Live on the industry sites: RAB.com, AllAccess.com, etc. for leads and available positions. If you decide on a career in sales, please understand that you will not be driving a BMW over night. It takes to time to develop a strong relationship with the "heavy hitters" in any market. You have to have a tough skin … rejection is just part of the game and you cannot take it personally. However, it is very rewarding to start working with a client from the ground level and watch his or her business grow, knowing that you played an active role in the success of his or her business.

Salary

New: $30,000 to $40,000. Established: Up to $150,000.

station may charge for advertising. A college degree isn't always required, but it is common for sales personnel to have a degree.

TRAFFIC DIRECTOR—The traffic director is responsible for preparing minute-by-minute schedules of what goes on the air, and then maintaining logs of what actually aired. This person, who is usually aided by traffic assistants, handles all schedule changes and ensures that all advertisements that have been sold are broadcast according to the client's contract. The traffic director effectively serves as the link between the sales and programming departments, thus keeping both areas informed about what commercial times are available.

GENERAL SALES MANAGER—The GSM leads the sales force, coordinating efforts between the national and local sales managers. They also supervise billing, oversee sales promotions campaigns, and develop sales goals. This person is ultimately responsible for obtaining enough advertising revenue to sustain the station's operations. Most general sales managers started as sales representatives and worked their way up to this position.

LOCAL SALES MANAGER—The LSM leads the sales force that concentrates on local advertisers, such as a local car dealership or a neighborhood deli. Since these businesses do not create their own radio ads, the local sales manager must work with developing concepts for local businesses, getting those ads produced, and on-air.

NATIONAL SALES MANAGER—The NSM leads the sales force that concentrates on national advertisers, such as Coca-Cola, General Motors, or Microsoft. Because most of the work is with nationwide companies, the national sales manager focuses primarily on receiving and placing previously produced advertisements.

SALES REPRESENTATIVE—The sales representative, also called account executive, may work for either the local or national sales manager. In addition to securing advertisers, the sales rep may also write and produce some local ads. The pay is often a base salary with a commission for the number of sales brought in.

SALES ASSISTANT—This position supports the sales staff and managers by handling much of the office work, including drafting proposals, which allows the sales staff to focus on meeting with clients and developing business.

ENGINEERING—To make sure the station does not violate government broadcasting regulations, as well as to ensure equipment is in good operating order, radio stations employ a chief engineer, who is often assisted by a team of engineers. They are responsible for maintenance, repairs, and installation of equipment. The head of the engineering department, the chief engineer, may be aided by a maintenance engineer. The maintenance engineer performs routine and preventive cleaning and repair of the station's equipment.

Audio Positions that Complement Video

One fallacy is that local radio stations are the sole source of employment within the audio realm. Fortunately for those seeking jobs, this is not the case. Radio is just one aspect of the audio field, with other aural positions available in film, video, multimedia, and webstreaming. Couple this with jobs in the music and recording industries, and the employment outlook for audiophiles is strong. It is vital, however, that those seeking employment look for opportunities beyond the AM and FM dials.

In the purest division, one can delineate non-radio employment possibilities by evaluating whether a particular job is in production or postproduction. Production entails microphone placement, audio recording, and mixing live audio at a music performance. Postproduction, however, is the manipulation of audio signals and tracks once they are already recorded onto a medium. Sound editing, copying compact discs, and mixing prerecorded dialogue tracks from a film shoot are examples of postproduction.

For production, the audio person has one overriding concern—to obtain the best audio recording possible. This is achieved through microphone placement, acoustical control, and maintaining correct audio-recording levels. In postproduction, the goal is to manipulate existing audio tracks into a desirable final format.

Audio Positions

ADR ARTIST—This person is responsible for replacing dialogue that was not cleanly recorded during the production process, through Automated Dialogue Replacement. ADR skills also come into play when dubbing foreign language films to English, and vice versa.

BOARD OPERATOR—Frequently referred to as a "board op," this position operates the audio console and other equipment in a control room during a broadcast or the recording of a production.

BOOM OPERATOR—This person operates the boom microphone during a broadcast or the recording of a production.

FOLEY ARTIST—This audio employee performs sound effects in a Foley studio. Here, the Foley Artist watches videos or films and mimics the actions on the screen, performing realistic sound effects for the final product.

PARABOLIC MIC OPERATOR—This person operates the parabolic microphone during the recording of a production. The parabolic mic operator is most popular at sports events, where the operator handles a clear parabolic dish, which resembles a small satellite dish. By pointing the center of the dish at the action, clear audio of the player on the field can be obtained.

Music Recording Industry

The advent of digital technology, affordable computers, burnable compact discs, and software such as Adobe Flash and Cool Edit has transformed the music recording and distribution industries. With a minimal investment and an acoustically acceptable recording space, virtually anyone can create recorded music for distribution.

The areas of employment are primarily in production, although the finished product will be sent to a distributor or a larger producer, who can then deliver the recorded tracks to a larger marker. Recording houses are also highly dependent on the community in which they are based. A recording house in a large city or one with a dedicated music background (such as Los Angeles, Nashville, or Austin) will have a better chance of working with musicians than a recording house in a rural area.

Music Recording Industry Positions

PRODUCER—Ultimately responsible for the finished sound, the producer does more than oversee the recording sessions. The producer is in charge of the record label, which includes dealing with singers and musicians, overseeing budgets, and scheduling the studio. The producer must also scout new artists, work with songwriters, and try to develop a group of talented performers under their label. At smaller, independent labels, a producer owns the recording studio. At larger labels, several producers work under the direction of a studio owner. There is no defined track to become a producer, as they can emerge from previous positions as engineers, composers, arrangers, studio musicians, artists, or managers.

RECORDING ENGINEER/MIXER—This person is in charge of placing the microphones, running the mixing board, and recording audio tracks for the producer and performers. With the new digital technology, some recording houses bypass analog audio tape in favor of recording into a computer. Regardless of the physical medium, the recording engineer must ensure a clean recording and mix of the audio work.

MASTERING ENGINEER—This person does their work during the final creative step in the recording process. The mastering engineer takes the tracks from the recording engineer and works with the producer and artists to create a master tape, from which the final compact discs will be copied.

Conclusion

While they are closely related, traditional radio positions and those in evolving audio fields provide different dynamics for potential employees. Business, technological, and consumer factors are altering the landscape of how listeners interact with radio, and the corresponding trend forecasts a decline in employment at traditional radio stations.

Audio fields, however, provide opportunities related to new technologies, the music industry, and visual media. Rather than focusing on the reduction of available jobs in the narrow field of radio, job seekers should concentrate their efforts on the broader industry of audio and the evolving employment positions that are available.

R-E-F-E-R-E-N-C-E-S

All About Broadcasting. The National Alliance of State Broadcasters Associations. 18 September 2008. <www.careerpage.org/joblist.php>

"Clear Channel Know The Facts." 18 Sept. 2008 <www.clearchannel.com/Corporate/corporate_ktf.aspx>

Crouch, Tanja. *100 Careers in the Music Business.* Barron's Educational Series, 2001.

Gerardi, Robert. *Opportunities in Music Careers.* VGM Career Books, 2002.

National Radio Format Rankings and Station Counts. "Radio Today 2008 Edition." Arbitron.com. <www.arbitron.com/downloads/radiotoday08.pdf>

Papper, Robert, "Seize the Pay," *RTNDA Communicator,* June 2007, p. 17.

"Sirius and XM Complete Merger." 29 July 2008 <http://xmradio.mediaroom.com>

U.S. Department of Labor, Bureau of Labor Statistics. Career Guide to Industries: Broadcasting. 2008 <www.bls.gov/oco/cg/cgs017.htm>

"Weekly Online Radio Audience Increase from 11 Percent to 13 Percent of Americans in Last Year." Arbitron.com. 9 April 2008. <www.onlinepressroom.net/arbitron/>

4 Television and Broadcast Video

The Dominance of Television

The impact of television continues to grow, with households consistently watching more TV programming. The Nielsen Company shows that the average U.S. household consumed 8 hours and 14 minutes of television viewing every day between September 2005 and September 2006. Many households have more than one television, and with the ever-expanding roster of cable and satellite channels, the number of employment opportunities continues to grow for both on-air and behind-the-scenes positions.

According to a media analysis from Veronis Suhler Stevenson, overall media usage is poised to increase. The 2010 projections estimate that consumers will watch 1,733 hours of television annually. To put that in perspective, the same study estimates overall media usage at 3,620 hours per year. This means television will command almost as many media hours as radio, music, print, videogames, and movies combined.

Further, the Bureau of Labor Services notes that 73 percent of workers within the broadcasting industry work in television and radio broadcasting, with 34 percent employed in radio and 39 percent in television. During the same year, the Bureau of Labor Statistics reports that broadcasting provided about 331,000 jobs, with most positions concentrated in larger stations in large cities.

Although television is a dominant information and entertainment medium with many establishments and employees, it is a highly competitive field for prospective workers. To better understand the employment possibilities, the realm of television stations can be divided into their television markets and networks.

Television Markets

Television markets are divided into 210 Designated Market Areas, or DMAs, in the United States. The number one DMA is New York, as market size is awarded based on the number of viewers a station reaches. New York boasts 7,391,940 television households, which is about 6.5 percent of all televisions in the country. The other top five markets are Los Angeles, with 5.6 million television households; Chicago, with 3.4 million; Philadelphia, with 2.9 million; and Dallas-Fort Worth, with just over 2.4 million. San Francisco–Oakland, Boston, Atlanta, Washington, D.C., and Houston round out the top ten.

The second tier of stations is known as the Top 50, including cities such as Kansas City, San Diego, Salt Lake City, and Las Vegas. Examples of Top 100 stations are Austin, Honolulu, and Springfield, Missouri.

Some markets are a combination of smaller cities, as the individual cities are not big enough to support TV stations by themselves. An example is Yakima-Pasco-Richland-Kennewick in southern Washington. Individually, these cities cannot generate enough sales revenue to support television stations. Collectively, they form the 126th market.

The smaller markets are in rural areas, often in the Upper Midwest or Alaska, where there simply are not many viewers. The smallest five markets are Helena, Montana (206), Juneau, Alaska (207), Alpena, Michigan (208), North Platte, Nebraska (209), and Glendive, Montana (210). Unlike the top DMAs, smaller markets do not have local affiliates for NBC, ABC, CBS, and FOX networks, since their towns do not have enough advertisers to support more than one station. Glendive, for example, only broadcasts to 3,890 households, targeting just 0.003 percent of the U.S. population.

These market rankings are fluid. In the top ten markets, Dallas–Fort Worth changed places with San Francisco-Oakland and Atlanta jumped over Washington, D.C. from the 2006–2007 and 2007–2008 Nielsen ratings. The moves can be more drastic in smaller markets, as a shift in population can alter the broadcasting landscape. Jackson, Mississippi, fell three positions to 90; Boise, Idaho, jumped five spots to 113; and Lima, Ohio, vaulted eleven spots to 185.

Most college graduates will start in a smaller market, although there are always exceptions to the rule. Starting in a Top 10 market is rare, while starting in the Top 100 is more realistic. Most employment opportunities will be in markets ranging from 50 down to 150. Markets smaller than 150 generally do not offer as many opportunities, as there are not as many network affiliates broadcasting in those towns.

Larger markets translate into larger paychecks for employees. According to the 2006 RTNDA/Ball State University Survey, news reporters in the top 25 markets earn $56,000 annually, while those in the smallest 60 markets pull in only $20,000 per year. Big market news directors make $115,000 per year, compared to $53,000 for their small-market counterparts. Across job descriptions ranging from assignment editors to sports reporters, those working in bigger newsrooms bring home two to three times more money than those in the small markets.

The Networks

As the television markets have a variety of network affiliates, the networks themselves also have jobs available. Working in a network headquarters entails moving to a large city, usually New York, Los Angeles, Washington, D.C., or Atlanta. Other opportunities are at their production facilities or major news bureaus in cities such as Chicago or Orlando.

Each major network is part of a different corporate family. News Corporation, for example, owns the Fox Network while the Walt Disney Company owns ABC Television. Every network has a searchable employment database on their website, as well as job postings from their individual affiliates across the country. Most also list their overseas opportunities.

The employment opportunities at the networks mirror those found at the individual stations with only a few differences. There tend to be more behind-the-scenes positions available, particularly on the technical side. Engineering staffs are much larger. There is also a greater need for those interested in the business side of the corporation.

One advantage of media consolidation is that it allows for career movement within a corporate structure. It is not uncommon for an employee to start at one channel of a corporation, such as working as an editor for TNT, and then move to a similar post at a different channel within the Time Warner organization. This pattern of mobility is also seen among news station owners, such as Cox Communications and Sinclair Broadcasting. These groups own the individual stations and sometimes give preference to applicants working within the corporation in a different market. For example, an employee at Sinclair's WTTA station in Tampa, Florida, with a proven record of accomplishment within the corporation, may have an advantage when an opening comes up at sister station WGME in Portland, Maine.

Salaries and Job Expectations

The 2007 Annual Survey of Journalism and Mass Communication Graduates surveyed 2,271 spring graduates from a probability sample of 83 universities across the nation. The average salary among respondents working in television was $29,300, while cable television employees earned $30,500. The survey also noted that job satisfaction among these workers was on the upswing; 42.1 percent of those surveyed said they were "very satisfied" with their job.

However, the job expectations for new employees are often inconsistent with what the employee had anticipated. As television is a 24-hour entity that must be sustained, entry-level positions are often overnight, weekend, or early morning shifts. Cub news reporters find themselves on call to cover spot news events. Programming events, such as "sweeps weeks" lend themselves to odd schedules, requiring workers to labor extra hours to promote the station. Seasonal work presents unusual hours, as veteran employees take off major holidays and summer vacations, leaving the newer workers to fill the void. Between lower-than-expected salaries, irregular working hours, and the lack of desirable on-air time, the turnover rate in television is high, particularly among those in their first years of employment.

Finally, the Bureau of Labor Statistics projects uneven employment possibilities at television stations through 2016. Positions for announcers are expected to drop almost 10 percent, by far the greatest drop in the industry. News reporters should gain 9 percent more jobs, videographers increase 6.6 percent, and film and video editors increase a mere 1%. Solid growth is foreseen in sales and related occupations, with an increase of 20.9 percent.

Television Station Positions

Television stations divide their employees among four areas: (1) news, (2) sales and traffic, (3) production, and (4) engineering. While many broadcast journalism graduates plan on news jobs, there are many more opportunities at the stations. Most employees of television stations are never seen on the air, but instead work in

Personal Profiles: *Josh Cook*

Name, title, place of employment, and city/state?

Josh Cook, Associate Producer with ESPN, mainly with *Jim Rome Is Burning* in Hollywood, California

Job duties

Finalizing graphics, editing highlights, b-roll, and correspondent pieces, and working as the Tape A.D. during live broadcasts.

What is a typical day like?

I get to work at 6:00 am and pull into the studio lot when it's dark. I get in and all the Associate Producers get together and delegate to the P.A.s to take in footage off the feed and Tivo of last night's action. We work on probable takes until we get scripts in around 8:30 am. At that point, we all go over the script, making sure that we have all the footage that we need and correcting any statistical errors that might have happened. I then take 30 minutes and make the specific take graphics. For example, if the Colts and Patriots are a take, I use Colts and Patriots helmets. Next, I head to the editing bays and work on bumps for each segment and the guest, and, if I have time, I knock out a take or two. Then, I work on the Roll-ins for the forum and guest segments, which is a combined six minutes of footage. Here comes the lay-off period where we lay all segments b-roll, bumps, and roll-ins onto digital beta tapes. While the tapes are laying off, as the Tape A.D., I log all the in-times, descriptions, total running times, and outs of each take and roll-in. We head to the control room at 12:50. The control room does a technical rehearsal of each segment with the playback reel and graphics. The show goes live at 1:30, 4:30 Eastern. While the show is going live, I count off the times of b-roll to the director. When the show ends, I either prepare for the next day's show with footage usage reports or I head to the edit bay and work on a correspondent piece for a couple hours. On average, I work an eleven-hour day with meals while I work.

How did you obtain your job?

I saw the posting of the job on entertainmentcareers.net. I submitted my résumé, and with my sports-covering experience, knowing Avid, and [knowing] Photoshop (a rare combination), they gave me a call. I came in for an interview and took a sports quiz ([scored] a 90) and sat down with an A.P. Then, in my second interview, they tested my Photoshop and editing abilities. Even though I came from a small school, I beat out Ivy Leaguers because I worked at my school's media center and taught myself Photoshop along with my editing knowledge from classes.

Salary

As an Associate Producer living in Hollywood (expensive place to live), I will make between $45,000 to $50,000 this year. Some of that comes from freelance work for the ESPY's and ESPN.

one of the other off-camera areas. Regardless of which of the four areas an employee works in, a member of management, such as these three primary positions, ultimately reviews their performance:

GENERAL MANAGER—The general manager is responsible for every aspect of a station's operation. This position requires business knowledge, leadership ability, and a technical understanding of how a station operates.

BUSINESS MANAGER—The business manager is responsible for all financial transactions. Business managers are generally expected to have extensive accounting and financial management experience.

STATION MANAGER—The station manager is the chief operating officer of the station and must have effective personnel management skills and a thorough knowledge of all aspects of broadcast operation.

Employment Forecasts

As the most prominent production within a local television station, the news department is an essential link to viewers. Given its visibility, many potential applicants target the news department first for employment. However, the Bureau of Labor Statistics forecasts mixed growth in this sector. The demand for reporters and correspondents will increase 9 percent through 2016, openings for camera operators will rise 6.6 percent, and producers and directors will gain 8.3 percent more jobs.

Other TV jobs show either minimal growth or an actual loss of jobs. Employment opportunities for film and video editors will increase a paltry 1 percent through 2016, while radio and television announcers will find 9.7 percent fewer jobs.

Conversely, there are still dynamic fields with impressive growth in television stations. Double-digit increases in jobs are forecast for those in sales (20.9 percent), multimedia artists and animators (24 percent) and computer specialists (24.4 percent).

News

ANCHOR—The news anchors are the public faces the news operation uses to convey its message. Although they are only seen on the news set for a half hour at a time, anchors are a guiding force in the newsroom, working with producers to shape the newscast. News anchors are typically former news reporters who have risen up through the ranks. For this position, anchors must possess exemplary reading skills, a strong on-camera presence, and have a thorough knowledge of the day's events.

When a reporter starts work as an anchor, it is not an automatic switch. A reporter will often receive the opportunity to anchor when the usual anchor is on vacation, during a weekend, or on a holiday. It's also common practice to hire a news reporter at an entry-level station where the reporter anchors the weekend newscasts, then serves as a reporter for three days a week (thus getting two weekdays, like Tuesday and Wednesday, off).

Anchors are the sole position in a newsroom where gender, age, race, and even hair color are factors of employment. Since many newscasts have two news anchors, news directors hire anchors with complementing looks, such as a younger black female paired with an older white male. For this reason alone, when considering an anchor job, one should evaluate the station's current anchors for balance and diversity.

Personal Profile: *Mickey Goodwin*

Name, job title, place of employment, and city/state?

Mickey Goodwin, TV News Anchor, KNWA-TV, Fayetteville, Arkansas

Job duties

Anchor 6 & 10 weekend newscasts, report for the 5, 6, 9, & 10.

What is a typical day like?

Rule #1. There is no such thing as a typical day. However, I am scheduled for 1:30 pm to 10:30 pm. At 2:00 pm, we have an afternoon staff meeting. The News Director, Assignment Editor, Producers, Anchors, Photogs, and Reporters discuss the events from the planner. We determine which reporters and photogs will team up. Stories are assigned, and live shots are configured. However, all of the plans can change at any given moment because of breaking news. You could very well be in the middle of an interview when you're asked to drop what you're doing and rush to a house fire on the other side of town.

How did you obtain your job?

I found this job by "accident." I was near the end of my contract with another affiliate in the Southeast. I really did not intend to leave my previous employer. However, on a whim, I sent out 5 tapes to see what kind of response I'd get from other stations. That "whim" led to 3 job interviews, and 2 job offers. One of which was in Northwest Arkansas. The News Director put together an amazing package that I could not refuse.

Job search tips, hints, advice, or anecdotes

Listen to your heart. Your gut instinct. It's like my Dad always said, "When in doubt. Don't." If you live by these words, then you'll never be left wondering "what if." Take advantage of every opportunity that lands at your feet—yet use plenty of caution and judgment when meeting people, conducting interviews, and applying for jobs. However, do not be afraid to take a deep breath, and a leap of faith. Just listen to what your heart tells you, and you'll land safely.

Salary

In this size market, you can expect to make the low-20s for a general assignment reporter. Anchoring will bring in a few more bucks. I'm nestled between $30 and $40K a year, but the News Director was able to work with me because I had so much experience coming in. I've been in the business for 10 years . . . and it has taken me this long to work my way up to this point. Good luck!

Like a news director, anchors bear a disproportionate burden of maintaining satisfactory ratings. If viewership slips, a news station may bring in consultants who direct the anchors to wear different clothing or try a different hairstyle. If ratings fall too far, anchors are often replaced.

ASSIGNMENT EDITOR—The assignment editor runs the assignment desk, which is the loudest and most energetic part of the newsroom. This person monitors

Personal Profile: *Lucas Johnson*

Name, job title, place of employment, and city/state?

Lucas Johnson, Director/Technical Director, WSB-TV, Atlanta, Georgia

Job duties

I usually TD for the 6 pm and 11 pm shows Sunday through Tuesday, as well as for the noon and 5 pm shows on Friday. I direct and TD the Saturday morning and noon shows. And I direct and TD our community show *People 2 People* and our weekly sports show *Sports Final*. I also edit our fish and game forecasts for air in various shows.

What is a typical day like?

Every day is different! However, during the week, I typically come in around 2:30. We have a meeting with the show producers and editors to talk about the day's shows and what might be needed in pre-production or special effects. The TD for the 5 pm show is in charge of pre-production for both the 5 pm and 6 pm shows. If that is me, I typically head into the control room around 3:30 to begin working on show preps. At 4 pm, we record a 4- to 5-minute mini-newscast for broadcast on our website. Around 4:10 pm, we do a 30-second news promo live that promotes the 5 pm newscast. At 4:30, we tape another 30-second promo, and a 15-second promo that master control will air between 4:30 and 5, promoting the 5 pm newscast. Then, I check all my equipment to make sure it is in proper working order, check to make sure all the pre-production video I was in charge of was properly filed for the show, and get ready for the show. Then, I "punch" the show from 5 to 6 pm. After that, another TD takes my place for the 6 pm show. We usually have a dinner break from 7:30–8:30 pm. Then we have a meeting at 9:00 pm to talk about what will be needed for the 11pm show. I usually go into the control room around 9:30 to begin pre-production for the 11. Then, at 10 pm, we rehearse our lottery drawing for the evening. Then we tape 35-second, 15-second, and 8-second news promos promoting the 11 pm show. I continue working on pre-production until 11. We typically do the lottery drawing live, right before the newscast, then run a :05 promo, then go right into the 11 pm show. At 11:30, the newscast is over, and I usually go home around 11:45!

How did you obtain your job?

I was a little unconventional. During spring break of my freshman year in college, I went around to all the news stations in Atlanta, handing out resumes, trying to get an internship for the following summer. I got a call-back from WSB, asking me to come in for an interview. I did my internship the summer after my freshman year, and was hired on as a freelance Production Assistant. I continued working as a freelance PA throughout college, working some weekends and holidays. During my senior year, I was a stringer for WSB and shot a few stories that aired on WSB-TV and CNN. After graduation, I was hired as a part-time robotic camera operator at WSB-TV. I did that for two years, and then was hired on full-time as a Technical Director.

Job search tips, hints, advice, or anecdotes

A Hollywood producer once told me, it's not about what you know, but who you know, which is partly true. Nevertheless, you really have to make your own

Personal Profile: *Lucas Johnson (continued)*

opportunities. If any job opportunity comes up, no matter how insignificant it sounds, take it. You may just be pulling cable for a commercial shoot, but you'll also be meeting people who know other people. As long as you show up on time, do your job to the best of your ability, and are persistent, people will remember you. Meeting contacts is paramount. I have a friend who was on a production site as a cable puller, when the Chyron operator didn't show up. When they asked if anyone had any Chyron experience, he said, "Sure, I do!" He had never seen a Chyron machine in his life. However, he sat down, figured out as much as he could, and he got his foot in the door as the go-to-guy.

Salary

Just under $50,000.

the police scanners, watches competing newscasts, reads wire feeds, serves as an instant resource for stories, and maintains files of news sources and story ideas. Not only does the assignment editor help the field crews develop stories, he or she also allocates news gear, vans, and personnel to cover stories. To help convey the variety of stories available to the producers on a given day, the assignment editor uses a large dry erase board, listing stories, crew, locations, times, and story status.

DIRECTOR AND TECHNICAL DIRECTOR—These people are responsible for the actual on-line execution of a program. They supervise production elements and the various control room and studio personnel. The crews they supervise are listed under the "Production" section of this chapter, as most crew members work on projects other than news during a typical day.

EDITOR—Editors work with producers, reporters, and writers to build news packages from the raw tape sent in from the field crews or gathered on feeds from networks or other sources. Many editing duties are now performed by videographers or, in some smaller markets, reporters.

MANAGING EDITOR AND EXECUTIVE PRODUCER—These positions are the second-in-command in the newsroom, answering to the news director. Often, these positions are combined and the titles are used interchangeably, but the job demands are the same, requiring more hands-on in daily newsroom operations. When the news director is unavailable, they decide the content of the overall newscast.

NEWS DIRECTOR—The news director is the ultimate authority to decide what stories are covered. Not only does the news director supervise a staff of reporters, producers, videographers, editors, writers, and the rest of the news crew, they also oversee the news budget and closely monitor what competing television stations are covering. Some news directors are only in the newsroom for a fraction of the day, with much of their time diverted in meetings, community functions, and administrative conferences. News directors typically work up to that position after serving as a news reporter, producer, or anchor. While the job is financially rewarding, the news director is often the first person blamed if the newscast slips in the ratings, thus the pressure to maintain market share is constant. At a large station, an assistant news director, who typically handles personnel and budget matters, aids the news director.

PRODUCER—There are two types of producers in television news, and both differ from producers in the video production realm or a typical movie producer. In television news, a producer may be dedicated to a single story, segment, or series, allowing the producer to focus on a specific task. In large markets, a producer may work with a reporter and videographer on a five-part series on homelessness or the county budget.

The other type of producer, who is found more commonly in smaller markets, is responsible for an entire newscast. Similarly, a station would have a morning show producer, another for the noon newscast, a 5 pm producer, a 6 pm producer, and an 11 pm producer. Whether a producer is responsible for a news story or an entire show, their mission is to create visual, informative programs out of interviews, scripts, and video footage. Their work is under constant deadline pressure.

REPORTER—The reporter is the key "front-line" person in the news department who must be on-the-scene at every kind of event. Local news reporters must be excellent writers, capable of working quickly and accurately to sum up the key elements of a news story and make it understandable and relevant to the audience. They cover local news, write news copy, and read it on-air. In smaller markets, they may also cover traffic, weather, or sports.

SPORTS—This can range from two or three people to an entire department, depending on market size. Sports personnel must have a clear understanding of sports, a commitment to work evenings and weekends when most sports events occur, and a personable on-air manner.

VIDEOGRAPHER—The videographer works alongside reporters to capture events on tape and to produce live, on-scene coverage of breaking news stories. In addition to operating the video camera and sound, electronic news gathering (ENG) crews must also operate sophisticated microwave and satellite transmission equipment to "feed" programming or news segments back to the studio from remote locations.

WEATHER—Meteorologists develop weathercasts for the local market and present them on-air. The difference between a meteorologist and a "weatherman" is based upon educational background and credentials.

The American Meteorological Society, the nation's premier professional organization for those in the atmospheric and related sciences, has three certification programs that recognize broadcast and consulting meteorologists who have achieved a certain level of competency: the Certified Broadcast Meteorologist (CBM) program, the AMS Seal of Approval, and the Certified Consulting Meteorologist program.

Meteorologists should complete the American Meteorological Society (AMS) Education Program to receive the AMS Seal of Approval. The AMS Seal was launched in 1957 as a way to recognize on-air meteorologists for their sound delivery of weather information to the public. Applicants without this industry-recognized seal will find their employment options severely restricted.

In 2005, the AMS introduced the Certified Broadcast Meteorologist (CBM) program. The main difference between the CBM and the AMS Seal of Approval is that CBM applicants must hold a college degree in atmospheric science or meteorology.

WRITER—The writer's responsibilities may include monitoring news feeds, preparing news packages for voicing by anchors or reporters, researching story information, booking guests for live interviews on news shows, and producing segments of news programs. Exceptional writing skills are necessary.

Sales and Traffic

GENERAL SALES MANAGER—The general sales manager (GSM) leads the sales force, coordinating efforts between the national and local sales managers. This person is ultimately responsible for obtaining enough advertising revenue to sustain the station's operations. Most general sales managers started as sales representatives and worked their way up to this position.

LOCAL SALES MANAGER—The local sales manager (LSM) leads the sales force that concentrates on local advertisers, such as local restaurants or a neighborhood dry cleaner. Since these businesses do not create their own radio ads, the local sales manager must work with developing concepts for local businesses, getting those ads produced, and getting them on-air.

NATIONAL SALES MANAGER—The national sales manager (NSM) leads the sales force that concentrates on national advertisers, such as Pepsi, Apple Computers, or Burger King. Because most of the work is with nationwide companies, the national sales manager focuses primarily on receiving and placing already-produced advertisements.

PROGRAM DIRECTOR—The program director works closely with the general manager and sales manager to determine and direct the station's policies and to plan the most effective program schedule for the station.

SALES REPRESENTATIVES—The sales representatives at a station may work for either the local or national sales managers. In addition to securing advertisers, they may also write and produce some local ads. The pay is often a base salary with commissions for the number of sales brought in.

TRAFFIC—The traffic department is responsible for preparing minute-by-minute schedules of what goes on the air, and then maintaining logs of what actually aired. The traffic coordinator, who is usually aided by traffic assistants, handles all schedule changes and ensures that all advertisements that have been sold are broadcast according to the client's contract.

Production

COMMUNITY RELATIONS DIRECTOR—The community relations director plans, coordinates, and executes a station's services and programs that are developed to respond to the needs of the community.

CONTINUITY WRITER—The continuity writer prepares some of the local commercial and promotional copy. In order to be successful, this person must be detail-orientated and have skills in computer and word-processing operations.

GRAPHIC ARTIST—A graphic artist supports all production activities. In addition to computer skills, a background in art, design, and radio-television production is valuable.

PRODUCER—The producer develops and organizes local programs and is responsible for scripting, story development, booking of guests, overseeing field production, and editing.

PRODUCTION ASSISTANT—A production assistant, or PA, works with all production personnel, helping where necessary.

PRODUCTION MANAGER—This position is responsible for all of the details required in the actual production of local programming. The production manager supervises producers, directors, floor directors, and stage managers.

PROMOTIONS DIRECTOR—The promotions director promotes the station's image, programs, and activities; conceives and executes a variety of written and taped station promotion spots; and secures station advertising in other media. In conjunction with the sales department, the promotions director develops ways to keep current viewers and advertisers and develops ways to attract new ones.

STAGE MANAGER—The director's representative on the studio floor and at the site of any live broadcast.

Personal Profile: *Kevin Allison*

Name, job title, place of employment, and city/state

Kevin J. Allison, Production Assistant, Fox Sports Net South, Atlanta, Georgia

Job duties

It varies, depending on the project that I am working on. For a special project such as the College Hoops Preview Shows, I may have more responsibilities placed on me because of the sheer mass of work that needs to be completed. During those shows, I worked with a team to complete 24 ACC and SEC Basketball Preview Shows. Because of such a strict deadline and everything that needed to be completed, I took on a segment of the show known as the "Conference Roundup" and stayed until 4 in the morning for two nights to complete that part of the show. This went along with putting together all four blocks of the show so it would be ready to Post. Job duties that I have had, again depending on the show or project, would be writing, editing, logging, making dubs, and being available for any request that my Producer might have.

What is a typical day like?

Again, it depends on the project that I am working on. For the College Hoops Previews, which lasted five weeks, there was not one well-defined day that was repeated throughout the process. For Pre-Production, I was responsible for making sure that all the tapes that would be needed were logged. Probably the greatest piece of advice I received while at my internship at MSGnetwork in New York was that time code is the most important thing in television. At the time, it kind of made me give [the person telling me] a second look. It is true, though. If the time code is not available for a piece of video that you need, then it is like finding a needle in a haystack. That is why logging is so important. When you are in production, you are building packages and blocks for the shows. As you get further and further along, you fine tune what you have completed to put a "look" on the video and whatever transitions and effects that are needed. During Postproduction, all the graphic pages and lower thirds are placed onto the video, and all blocks are seamed together.

How did you obtain your job?

Having the internship at MSGnetwork in New York helped get me interviews with some networks. I interviewed over at Turner Sports for a job that in the end was given to someone else. The producer I interviewed with contacted someone he knew here at FSN South, and I was brought in for an interview. Once it was determined that the College Hoops Preview Shows were going to take place, I was brought on board. I was pretty lucky to have that as my first project.

Job search tips, hints, advice, or anecdotes

It is extremely important to have experience in the field. My advice would be to know where you want to work. Do everything possible to do an internship at that network. It is the best way to get your "foot in the door" as everyone says.

Salary

I get paid on an hourly basis with overtime after 40 hours a week.

Personal Profile: *Kylie Mitchell*

Name, job title, place of employment, and city/state?

Kylie Mitchell, Project Coordinator, Home Shopping Network, St. Petersburg, Florida

Job duties

I help prepare and put together products for on air shows. Mostly, I focus on electronics and NFL, but I also have to prep cosmetics, knives, rugs, and dolls. Basically anything that takes a long time to get ready, I prep.

What is a typical day like?

On a typical day, I come in and find out what I will be working on that day. I print out any information and read any notes on that product. I usually get to work with other people, so it's pretty fun most of the time. Some days are very busy, and some days are very slow. A few times a week I have to help out the Backstage Coordination, which is what I used to do. They do the actual live show . . . switching products out and making them look nice. They also have to deal with hosts and guests, which can be quite stressful at times. My position now is much more relaxed and fun.

How did you obtain your job?

I got the job by simply applying. I actually applied for a more difficult position, and since I was under qualified, they offered me this one.

Job search tips, hints, advice, or anecdotes

The only job search advice I can offer is to start early, and apply to A LOT of places. Get as much experience as you can while in school or interning. Also, as always . . . contacts are very important.

Salary

I make $12 an hour which I think is somewhere in the $25K to $27K range. However, there is a lot of overtime opportunity at HSN, so I take advantage of that quite often (time and a half is great money). So I'd say I will make around $30,000 in a year.

Engineering

CHIEF ENGINEER—To make sure the station does not violate government broadcasting regulations, as well as to ensure equipment is in good operating order, radio stations employ a chief engineer, who is often assisted by a team of engineers. They are responsible for maintenance, repairs, and installation of equipment.

MAINTENANCE ENGINEERS—Maintenance engineers are responsible for the repair, maintenance, installation, and modification of all of the electronic equipment in the station.

MASTER CONTROL/VIDEOTAPE ENGINEER—This position is responsible for operating the videotape recording and playback equipment for live programs and during commercial breaks in network and taped shows.

STUDIO ENGINEER—This person is responsible for operating all of the equipment necessary for the production of a program, including the studio cameras, the audio console, studio lighting, the video switcher, and in some stations, the character generator and the electronic still-storage graphics display equipment.

Conclusion

Job opportunities at local television stations are uneven. The greatest growth is among positions that require computer/multi-media skills, and engineering degrees. Although the sales force will remain highly competitive, it will witness growth in the next decade.

For those who wish to work in the high-profile news division, jobs will be available for candidates who demonstrate persistence, applicable job skills, and the ability to shift from one job category to another. Reporters may become anchors or producers, while videographers will likely overlap with video editors. Except for heavily unionized news departments, such job shifts are to be expected.

Given the varying degrees of prospective job growth and declining rates at local television stations, potential employees should look beyond the typical on-air positions for employment. Industry consolidation, a greater reliance on computer interaction, and the phasing out of niche positions such as announcers and editors, will lead to keen competition in television.

REFERENCES

"All About Broadcasting." *Career Page.* The National Alliance of State Broadcasters Associations. 18 Sept. 2008 <www.careerpage.org/joblist.php>

American Meteorological Society. 15 Sept. 2008 <www.ametsoc.org/amsedu/>

Ellis, Elmo. *Opportunities in Broadcasting Careers.* VGM Career Services, 1999.

Fischer, David. *The 50 Coolest Jobs in Sports.* ARCO Thomson Learning, 2001.

Inside TV Ratings, Nielsen Media Research. 15 Sept. 2008. <www.nielsenmedia.com>

Media Usage and Consumer Spending: 2000–2010. U.S. Census Bureau, www.census.gov. VSS (Veronis Suhler Stevenson) Communications Industry Forecast, New York.

Nielsen Reports Television Tuning Remains at Record Levels. The Nielsen Company, 17 Oct. 2007, accessed 18 Sept. 2008 <www.nielsenmedia.com>

Noronha, Shonan. *Careers in Communications.* 4th ed. VGM Career Books, 2005.

Papper, Robert. *Seize the Pay*, RTNDA Communicator, June 2007, pp. 16–24.

Tucker, Lee B., and Tudor Vlad. "2007 Annual Survey of Journalism and Mass Communication Graduates." Annual Surveys of Journalism and Mass Communication. <www.grady.uga.edu/annualsurveys/Archive_News/Archive_News_15.php>. 18 Sept. 2008.

U.S. Department of Labor, Bureau of Labor Statistics. Career Guide to Industries: Broadcasting. 2008.

5 Corporate Media and Non-Broadcast Media

Introduction

There are many diverse occupations and career opportunities under the designation of Corporate and Non-Broadcast Media. In the corporate world, or private sector, there is a need for media producers in the technical and creative areas of production. Whether it is a large in-house media group, small in-house group, outside production company, or freelance, there is a demand for media services in the corporate arena. With the advent of digital technologies and inexpensive media production equipment, there is a great emphasis and need for producers, directors, multimedia artists, and a host of other creative and technical personnel.

The term corporate production often connotes the antiquated training and instructional films of the 1950s and 1960s. In those days, the sophistication of media production was vastly limited in technique and creativity, offering little in the way of narrative development and production technique. The objective was clear and unwavering in the dissemination of the subject or information that was provided. Initially used extensively by the military, these became known as "industrials" and were produced and utilized by big business beginning in the 1970s (DiZazzo, 2000). Usually shot on 16-millimeter film, these productions proved effective but too costly for smaller businesses.

It was not until the development of portable video formats that corporate production became cost effective and viable. Videotape did not require expensive developing and lab processing costs for the final production. Camcorders were self-contained and did not require separate sound recording systems for sync sound. It was also much easier to edit videotape and incorporate graphics and effects without the additional costs associated with film production. Even if film is utilized as the originating medium, the project can be inexpensively transferred to video format for editing and final dissemination. As videotape players and recorders became commonplace, it was far easier and more effective to distribute and duplicate a training, informational, or promotional production.

With digital technologies and the Internet, it is essential that all industries develop some form of multimedia or web presence for their survival. As with broadcasting programming, alternate forms of media delivery such as the Internet and wireless devices are now common and are expected for final delivery of content. In addition to new forms of delivery and dissemination, these technologies are also incorporated in internal communications and organizational training initiatives. The role of corporate production has vastly expanded from the short training films or "industrial" days to a rich and sophisticated media environment. The use of media in the corporate world has expanded to include training programs on the

World Wide Web, promotional DVDs at the point of purchase, websites for customer information and promotion, and many other creative solutions. The use of digital and multimedia applications is virtually limitless in the corporate production world.

In pursuing employment in the corporate media world, there are more opportunities today than in the past. As previously stated, traditional corporate media production was limited to occupations that required specific skills in the area of film and video production. As multimedia technology continues to expand and creative uses of these new technologies serve this industry, the occupations are becoming more varied and diverse. The one caveat concerning this change in the industry is the ability to multitask and function in various production capacities. One of the consequences of the increased use of multimedia technology is that traditional production roles are consolidating. One of the hallmarks of digital technology is the ease of use and ability to perform multiple functions and tasks. Computer editing and graphics programs can produce sophisticated projects that formerly required a team of creative and technical personnel. By utilizing new technologies, the delivery of content via the Internet or DVD offers greater interactivity, and thus greater usefulness and effectiveness. In particular, training and point-of-purchase materials are now produced with interaction features. Instead of creating several linear programs, Internet and DVD materials allow for menus features and selection of specific programs. For training materials, this allows for question and answer sections based on the interactive design of non-linear delivery systems.

In-House Media Groups

Large In-House Production Departments

The use of media has become a necessity for doing business in modern society. Given this premise, many large corporations have established in-house production departments. The size and sophistication of these in-house production groups vary greatly. The initial investment can vary greatly depending on the number of creative and technical personnel and facilities to fulfill a company's media needs and objectives. For larger in-house production groups, these departments often require tremendous resources and investment in equipment, production facilities, and personnel. With the ever-increasing dependency on the use of media for training, information, and promotion, it is often cost effective to make the investment in a self-contained production facility.

Within these large in-house groups, there is a great need for support and creative occupations. For creative services, there are writers, directors, editors, graphic artists, multimedia artists, web developers, and a host of other creative personnel. For technical and support services, there are production managers, producers, engineers, cinematographers, and other production support personnel. It is common to contract many of these service occupations on a per-use basis. These temporary employees are referred to as freelance personnel. As with other areas of media production, many of the personnel needed to staff and manage a production are freelancers.

Large in-house departments are supported by the other departments or clients within the company or corporation. A production manager or head of the production unit will coordinate and budget each project. The cost of a project is then passed on to the department or unit initiating the project or production. In order to

Personal Profile: *Evans Wilson*

Name, title, place of employment, and city/state?

Evans Wilson, Video Training Coordinator, Weatherford, Houston, Texas

Job duties

To make training videos for engineers by filming and editing the assembly, disassembly, and operation of oil well tools. Recently, I have been helping a lot in making simple 3D animations for interactive online training, and even incorporating these into the videos.

What is a typical day like?

I've only been with the company about 7 months now and a lot of that time we have spent trying to build up this new in-house video department. Until I am classified to be on real oilrigs, I do my shooting at a test rig/training facility. I will take that footage back to the office and edit it sometimes alongside an expert on the tool or curriculum person to create a video product. Most of my days are spent editing and future planning with bosses.

How did you obtain your job?

My uncle works for Halliburton (a competing oil company). He was able to get me an internship at Stonehenge Productions here in Houston (a production company that specializes in video, staging, and animation for oil companies). This was during the summer before my last semester at Valdosta. Shortly after I graduated, I got a call from my internship offering me an opportunity to work for one of their clients, Weatherford, who was looking for a creative young video graduate.

Job search tips, hints, advice, or anecdotes?

Network! Get your name in with your friend's friend's dad, or whomever you have a connection to that might have a job in your field. If you get an opportunity, make yourself a strong asset. Don't burn any bridges. Also, squeeze in an internship before you graduate.

Salary

I make around $60,000 annually.

subsidize the large investment in these expensive groups, a corporation will often allow the department to contract works out to external clients. These services may include the use of the production facilities, creative services, editing, or oversight of an entire campaign or production. Depending upon the productivity and use of the facilities, large in-house groups have the potential to be profitable entities. In addition to offering a return on the initial investment, large in-house groups may offer steady employment for part-time and freelance workers.

Other factors that benefit a corporation in developing a large in-house group include consistent and reliable production support, manageable production costs, and lastly, an opportunity to generate revenue through the production services. Since developing an internal media group is usually seen as a cash or revenue drain on a company, the advantages and disadvantages of doing so are carefully weighed. In recent years, large in-house groups have decreased due to the proliferation and convergence of digital technologies. Many smaller production companies and free-lance production personnel are ambitious and skilled while offering a cost-effective alternative to a large initial investment for facilities, personnel, and equipment.

Small In-House Production Departments

Smaller in-house groups usually consist of the creative personnel and contract labor to provide production services and facilities. Often part of a larger company, these small in-house groups manage a corporation's media needs without the enormous investment in facilities or large production and support staff. In some cases, small media departments have lower cost portable digital video equipment. With the advent of MiniDV and tapeless digital formats, companies are now able to purchase broadcast quality production equipment for a nominal investment. In addition to low-cost field production equipment, the cost to edit has also benefited from the digital revolution. With a computer, video card, and low-cost editing software, companies are able to complete productions with very little investment in editorial equipment. The conver-gence of media and the increasing sophistication of computer processing and soft-ware contribute to a decline in the costs of both equipment and personnel.

These facts can seem detrimental to overall growth in occupations in the cor-porate media world. In reality, however, lower production and equipment costs offer companies an incentive to utilize media for their needs in training, promotion, and information. For this reason, there is an increase in small in-house groups within the corporate world. Many industries now see the necessity of hiring media personnel within the corporate structure. These creative teams develop projects, serve as writers, producers, directors, and often as the crew and editor on the pro-duction. If there is a need to produce a project beyond the capabilities of the core group, there are ample outside production companies and support personnel in the freelance world. In addition to the production personnel, studio rental and location shooting are alternatives to investing in large and expensive production facilities.

Overall, small in-house production groups seem to benefit companies greatly. In addition to lower personnel, equipment, and facilities costs, there is the advan-tage of having professional media support within the company. This allows for con-sistent production value, manageable costs, and timely completion of productions. Since large in-house media groups are becoming scarce, there are more opportuni-ties for employment in small in-house media departments.

Production Companies

As previously stated, production companies are often contracted to serve the media needs of corporations. Some corporations do not have in-house media personnel, and choose to contract production services externally. Production companies operate on a contractual basis. As in the motion picture industry, a production company often spe-cializes in a certain type of production. Many commercial production companies are set up well to serve the needs of the corporate world. In addition to commercial pro-duction companies, there are companies that specialize specifically in serving the needs of corporations. These companies often produce programs specifically for internal company dissemination, and not for public consumption. The costs for this type of production are often lower than the commercial production entities.

Personal Profile: *Emily Harp*

Name, job title, place of employment, and city/state?

My name is Emily Harp and I'm the owner of Shining Star Media in Valdosta, Georgia.

Job duties

As a small business owner, I do everything. I shoot weddings, performances, events, interviews, etc., usually with a second person running a camera. I do all of the editing, and I then design, build, and package the DVDs. I market my business through my website, bridal shows, and word of mouth. My business-minded husband makes sure we get the tax forms in on time and oversees the financial side of things (in his free time, ha ha) leaving me free to do what I love: "be creative."

What is a typical day like?

I work from my home and as a mother of a preschooler, a typical "work day" is difficult to define. I don't have set business hours. I take work calls as they come in. I get the most editing done when my child is in preschool or taking a nap. We adjust our schedule accordingly as jobs come up. It's extremely flexible and I love it.

How did you obtain your job?

I got my dream job right out of college as an editor for Bright Blue Sky Productions in Macon, Georgia. I was working for my hero-turned mentor and talked to him about starting my own small business on the side, something completely different than the high-end projects Bright Blue Sky produced. My boss was supportive and even helped me pick out the equipment that would best suit me in my venture. My husband and I have moved several times since that first job but my experience there taught me so much as an editor and fueled my passion for what I do. Now my business goes where I go.

Job search tips, hints, advice, or anecdotes?

If there is someone whose work you admire, do everything you can to train under them. Don't be afraid to start something on your own, just research, research, research!

Salary

My salary completely depends on the project. It could be anywhere from $500 to $2,500.

Production companies can provide a host of services and support to the corporate world. These companies may provide services and creative personnel in writing, directing, multimedia development, or editing. They may also offer production support in facilities such as location shooting, studio rental, editorial services, and production equipment rental. By providing this support and service, the contracting company is not responsible for the enormous initial investment in infrastructure, and only pays for services needed.

Corporations contracting services from a production company will usually rely on a coordinator within the company, or a freelance production coordinator or producer. These people are responsible for finding a company to service the corporation at a competitive price and in an efficient manner. Drawing on information about the specific media needs of the project, a coordinator or producer chooses and contacts an appropriate production company. It is also common for production companies to provide this type of production support or service.

Independent production companies benefit from the decline in large in-house media groups, since as the demand for small in-house media support declines, there will be an increase in occupational opportunities at those companies. Lower-cost digital technologies have benefited these production companies and the services they can offer and provide. The occupational outlook for these companies is increasing for new media and convergent media while the traditional media service occupations are less viable in the production support area of corporate media. As a benefit to students in college media programs, there are many worthy programs that teach digital and convergent media as part of their curriculum. Students in these programs are at an advantage for these career opportunities, but should be aware that they will continue to see a decline in traditional media occupations.

Freelance Occupations

As with many other areas of media production, freelance occupations play an increasingly important role in the production industries. As with the motion picture industry, most production personnel in the corporate media industry are employed on a freelance or temporary basis. Freelance occupations are responsible for much of the creative and technical support required during a production. These occupations include writers, directors, producers, multimedia and graphic artists, editors, location scouts, set dressers, engineers, and a variety of other production support positions. Freelance personnel are cost effective and necessary in the production of corporate media outside of large in-house media groups (DiZazzo, 2000). In addition to paying on a per use basis, freelance personnel often lend support or offer access to production equipment, locations, and facilities. Their salaries and rates are often open to negotiation, which is an additional benefit to the employing corporation. One drawback is that in times of high production, there may be a shortage of skilled and consistent production personnel. Regardless, many of the media production industries rely heavily upon the employment of freelance or temporary workers.

For students in college media programs, freelance employment offers an opportunity for entry-level work in the media production world. In particular, corporate media is rife with opportunities for students in college media programs. Often, corporate media productions are utilized for internal company purposes, and the expectation regarding the quality or program content is in line with the program objective. Broadcast quality is often sacrificed for lower production costs—in particular, when the objective of the production is to train or inform corporate employees of company procedure or policy. Lastly, the corporate world, in general, expects post-secondary education training of their employees. There is a fundamental difference when compared to other media production environments. As a student in a college media program, graduates have a considerable advantage to their less formally educated, yet skilled, counterparts.

Corporate and Non-Broadcast Groups	Occupational Outlook
Large In-House Production Departments	Declining
Small In-House Production Departments	Declining
Outside Production Companies	Increasing
Freelance Occupations	Increasing

Corporate Production

Training Productions

The training production is one of the most common uses of corporate media. These productions are used in teaching safe and proper usage of equipment and machinery, sales and motivational techniques, new equipment operations, and many other objectives related to a particular industry or company. Training productions are almost always intended for internal dissemination. The program structure for these productions is minimal, as they must be easy to comprehend and follow. Without elaborate or sophisticated production techniques, there is little need for extensive production personnel. The production personnel required to produce this type of project is similar to Electronic News Gathering (ENG) or newsgathering operations. Often, a camera operator, sound mixer, producer, and talent are sufficient to produce training productions.

Training productions present good opportunities for entry-level personnel to prove their merit or abilities. As corporate media continues to contract or outsource, freelance personnel and college media students are in prime positions to gain relevant experience in the production environment. An additional benefit to media students is that college and university media departments are often approached to supply production personnel for this type of production.

Promotional Productions

Promotional productions tend to be more sophisticated, and savvier, than their training counterparts. These productions are often used as point-of-purchase marketing to show ease of use, innovation, or versatility of a product or service. In addition, these productions may also be utilized to explain the use or assembly of the product to the consumer. Since this type of production is intended for limited public dissemination, the production value and technique must be of broadcast quality. It must engage or entertain the viewer but also offer enough relevant information to fulfill the objective of the promotion. As the demand for greater sophistication and entertainment value increases, the demands for creative and technical personnel are greater. Now that these promotional videos are finding audiences on the Internet with services such as YouTube, creative teams are adapting to new techniques and considerations for delivering content. In addition to the field production personnel outlined in the training production section, greater emphasis is placed on the creative and content development personnel.

As with the training production, there are many occupational opportunities in this type of production. Entry-level production personnel are not often considered in developing promotional productions, which usually require greater skill and expertise in media production. In most cases, entry-level production personnel must establish a track record or prove their ability in the production environment before producing promotionals. As with training productions, corporations continue to contract or outsource these productions, which increases opportunities for freelance and temporary production personnel.

Production Designations and Descriptions

Corporate Media Production

A list of occupations in corporate media is detailed below. The positions are general descriptions of production personnel utilized in all areas of corporate media production. The categories are separated into (1) preproduction, (2) production, and (3) postproduction groupings.

Preproduction

PRODUCER—The producer develops the project and coordinates the day-to-day operations and logistics of a production. This person is responsible for communications between the various entities or departments within or outside of the corporate structure. The producer oversees all aspects of the project including the creative, financial, and technical aspects, and ensures the production is completed on time and on schedule. There are different types of producers as they assume various responsibilities in the coordination and production of the project. Some designations in this occupation include: Executive Producer, Associate Producer, Line Producer, and Producer Manager.

ASSISTANT DIRECTOR—The Assistant Director assists the producer in handling logistical details related to the production of corporate media. The assistant director is an intermediate between the director, producer, and production personnel; he or she reports to the producer.

WRITER—Writers develop an idea or concept into a script for corporate production. The writer works closely with the producer and director to develop the project, and is often knowledgeable of the product or service. As with other types of production, the script will usually go through several revisions before it is ready for the production phase.

Production

DIRECTOR—The director oversees the overall creative aspects of a production. The director is responsible for interpreting the written script and executing it into a finished product. This person interacts with all technical and creative personnel under the financial and scheduling supervision of the producer.

CINEMATOGRAPHER—The cinematographer, or DP (Director of Photography), works under the direct supervision of the director. It is the cinematographer's responsibility to translate the director's vision into photographic or electronic imaging. Use of light and color, camera movement, and coordination of the camera personnel are all responsibilities of the cinematographer.

CAMERA CREW—Within the camera staff, there are: first and second camera assistants, camera operators, gaffers, and grips. Each position has its specific responsibilities and tasks. The camera assistants are responsible for the assembly, loading, and maintenance of the camera. The camera operator controls the camera during filming or taping. Gaffers are electricians responsible for the placement and maintenance of the lighting. Working under the supervision of the cinematographer, a gaffer performs the logistics of lighting the shot. Grips are supervised by the gaffer, and assist with the lighting process.

VIDEO ENGINEER—The video engineer oversees all technical video operations for television studio productions. A highly complex and sophisticated facility, the television studio requires an expert to coordinate and calibrate the highly technical equipment.

SOUND MIXER—The sound mixer or recordist is responsible for capturing production audio for the project. It is the mixer's responsibility to determine the best approach and technique to improve or alter the sound quality.

BOOM OPERATOR—The boom operator works in conjunction with the sound mixer to place the microphone on axis or in a position that best captures the dialogue, ambient audio or action of the shot.

ACTORS—Actors, or talent, portray the characters or serve as hosts in media productions. Typically, actors audition for the part and are selected by the producer and director. Most actors are represented by a facilitator known as an AGENT. The agent is usually contacted by the producer or CASTING DIRECTOR, and arranges for the actor to audition for a role in the production. It is the casting director's responsibility to contact agents and coordinate the audition process. In corporate media production, actors are often amateur or first-time actors. In some situations, actors in corporate media productions are actual employees of the company.

Postproduction

EDITOR—The editor selects the best shots and performances and assembles the material in a logical sequence. In consideration of the script or concept of the production, the editor is given creative liberty to discern what is aesthetically valued. While not fully autonomous in the editorial creative process, an editor is valued for the ability to approach the material with a fresh perspective. This creative process is overseen by the producer and often the director. It is the responsibility of the editor to maintain the director's vision and intent of the story.

ASSISTANT EDITOR—Within the editorial staff, there are support positions in the postproduction process, referred to as assistant editor.

AUDIO EDITOR or ENGINEER—The audio editor or engineer supervises the postproduction audio processes. These processes include automatic dialogue replacement (ADR), Foley, scoring, insertion of soundtrack, and the final mixdown of the entire audio sequence.

MULTIMEDIA ARTIST and ANIMATOR—Multimedia artists and animators occupations are often utilized throughout the production and postproduction processes. As computer and digital technologies become more essential to create media projects, the demand for skilled computer technicians and artists will be greater. While the demand for multimedia artists is great, it is also contingent upon the concept or need of the production.

PRODUCTION ASSISTANT—Support occupations are greatly needed in all phases of the production process. Within every area and department, there is a need for production assistants. These entry-level positions support and assist production personnel in every capacity. The responsibilities for this occupation vary greatly. As utility personnel, production assistants are required to work long hours, and are expected to perform onerous tasks. As a benefit to this position, production assistants are capable of gaining valuable on-the-job experience and opportunities for upward mobility.

Television Studio Productions

Within television occupations, there are many occupations related to studio production operations. These occupations are listed below.

TECHNICAL DIRECTOR—The technical director (TD), also known as the switcher, does the actual editing of shots in a television studio. The TD selects the shots specified by the director. In addition, the TD operates the production switcher, which is a highly complex and technical piece of equipment. The production switcher generates graphics, superimpositions, keys, and other picture effects.

FLOOR DIRECTOR—The floor director, or stage manager, is in charge of every operation on the studio floor. This includes set changes, cueing talent, and relaying the director's cues and shots. The Floor Director also supervises the operation of the teleprompter.

TELEPROMPTER—The teleprompter operator controls the prompting system made up of a pane of glass over the camera's lens that projects the script or narration for the talent. It is used so that the talent can look directly into the camera while addressing the viewers.

Production Designations	
Preproduction	Producer Assistant Director Writer
Production	Director Cinematographer Camera Crew Video Engineer Sound Mixer Boom Operator Actor Technical Director Floor Director
Postproduction	Editor Audio Engineer Multimedia Artist or Animator
All Phases	Production Assistant

Conclusion

Corporate media is an industry in transition, and the future of corporate media production is uncertain. In fact, the only certainty may be that the industry will continue to transform as media technologies converge and expand. The consolidation of production occupations and the growing outsourcing of corporate media production translate to a wealth of opportunities for ambitious and resourceful production employees. Whether the industry will shift from small in-house groups to independent production companies is unknown at this time. However, the fact remains that freelance and temporary employment positions are fast becoming the standard in the corporate media industry. With the increase in the use of technology, more advanced skills for digital media production are highly sought and valued. Lastly, corporate media production offers many opportunities to entry-level production personnel and students of college media programs.

REFERENCES

DiZazzo, Ray. *Corporate Media Production,* Focal Press, 2000.

Medoff, Norman, and Kaye, Barbara. *Electronic Media: Then, Now, and Later,* Boston: Allyn and Bacon, 2005.

"Occupational Employment Projections to 2010." U.S. Department of Labor, Bureau of Labor Statistics, 2008.

Zettl, Herbert, *Video Basics 5,* Wadsworth Publishing, 2006.

CHAPTER

6 Motion Pictures

Introduction

The motion picture industry includes feature film, commercial, and music video production. In addition, many of the programs on television are produced by the motion picture industry. Although it is largely based in Los Angeles, there are smaller production centers throughout the United States. The workforce is relatively small (about 357,000 people), but there are many diverse and varied trades within this industry, according to the Bureau of Labor Statistics (2008).

Several large studios control a large portion of the motion picture industry. Although these studios no longer directly produce film or video productions, they still control distribution and promotion of the final product. The studios, in effect, are responsible for the financing and overall control of the final media production. In the past, the major studios were vertically integrated, controlling and employing everyone involved in the production of motion pictures, including everyone from the executive producer of a film to the person who sold popcorn in a cinema. The old studio systems were efficient and profitable, but this control of the production process was considered monopolistic, and eventually needed to be dispersed into separate companies and areas of responsibility.

Occupations in the motion picture industry are highly specialized and require training beyond the bachelor's degree level. Given the structure of film production, technical knowledge and experience is often required to secure a position in the industry. Although a post-secondary education is preferred, it is not required given the complexity and requisite skill of the overall industry. Apprenticeships and on-the-job training are more common paths to secure a technical position in the production of motion pictures. The technical production and business side of the motion picture industry require different types of qualifications. On the production side, the emphasis is more on experience, while on the business side (which includes production management, producing, promotions, and general studio operations), candidates are expected to have a college degree. The preferred training for these areas is in business, law, and communications. An emphasis on technical film and video production are useful but not necessary. To understand these different types of occupations, it is helpful to know the difference between what is referred to in the industry as above-the-line and below-the-line positions.

Above the line and below the line refers to the actual budget of a motion picture production. Each occupation specific to a production is given a line item in the budget and are separated by this distinction. Above-the-line costs usually refer to costs based on creative services with compensation based on percentages. Above-the-line positions entail contributions to the production that are more difficult to assess specifically the actual amount of time or number of hours on the job. These positions, which are critical to the success and financial outcome of a production, are a way of ensuring ownership and oversight of the overall creative process. Some positions that are customarily designated as above-the-line are the director, writers, executive producer and sometimes the producer, line producer(s), and associate producer(s) (Bernstein, 1988).

Below-the-line costs are fixed personnel costs based on specific and defined production roles and time spent working. These positions are clearly defined and oriented to specific disciplines or areas of expertise. Many of these positions do not require a post-secondary education but require years of on-the-job training or apprenticeships. Many of these production roles are not permanent employment positions. They are referred to as "freelance" positions in the production environment. The exception to this nonpermanent status is the production of episodic or weekly television shows that are contracted by the networks or studios. In these situations, the below-the-line positions are contracted for the run of the series or at the discretion of the producers. It should also be clear that, at any point, the above-the-line personnel have the discretion or liberty to replace below-the-line personnel within the confines of the employment contract or union concerns. Some positions that are designated as below-the-line are assistant director(s), camera operator(s), sound mixer, gaffer, grips, make-up, wardrobe, property master, editorial, assistant and other production services required for completion of a production (Bernstein, 1988).

In both above-the-line and below-the-line, many of these positions have established guilds, unions and societies. These organizations are specific to certain areas of expertise, and require varying degrees of on-the-job performance or time spent working to become a member. In many situations, joining a guild, union, or society is by invitation only and is a requirement to work in the industry. Local and state employment laws govern these rules or requirements.

Feature Film Production

A producer is responsible for initiating a feature film production. The producer is then responsible for assembling the production team and financing the production (Bernstein, 1988). This type of producer is often given the title of Executive Producer. The project may be initiated or coordinated by one of the major studios, a production company, an independent producer, or, in rare cases, an individual. A feature film project is similar to any business endeavor; it starts with a business plan, financing, and an idea. As soon as the concept or script and finances are secured, a production team is put into place.

Preproduction

The beginning of the production process is referred to as the development or pre-production phase. This is usually the longest part of the production cycle, and often the most expensive. It is also the most volatile stage of production, and the project can fall apart at any time. As the planning for a feature film is both intense and time consuming, it requires organized and qualified personnel to handle the operations. This area of the production process is often the most rewarding in terms of financial compensation and requires greater aptitude, diversity, and analytical abilities. Many of these positions in the development process are contractual, above-the-line

Personal Profile: *Crystle Robertson*

Name, title, place of employment, and city/state?

Crystle Robertson, 24 years, Freelance Filmmaker/ Director, Atlanta, Georgia

Job duties?

In the freelance world of filmmaking, my jobs vary from project to project. I started as a Set Production Assistant (which is the usual entry-level position) on feature films, which required me to do many different tasks to ensure that the film crew was a well-oiled machine. I have also worked in the capacity of Production Coordinator, Director's Assistant, Director, Producer, and Executive Producer.

What is a typical day like?

The typical day is no less that 10 to 12 hours and varies in location and time. Some days we may start at dawn and work until night, some days we start in the evening and work until morning. The locations vary also. You may be on top of a mountain one day and be on the beach the next. It is a day full of problem solving and hustle. Production Assistants are expected not to sit down or appear tired at any point during the 12-hour shift. They usually help communicate the course of the day to the entire crew (i.e., they yell "Rolling!" very loud before the camera rolls to make sure no one talks during the take, they tell the crew "we are moving to scene 3 next" or "we have one more scene before we shoot outside").

How did you obtain your job?

I began with an internship on a movie. I called the production office to see if they needed any extra help and then told them that I would work for free. Many low-budget movies need additional help but do not have the money to pay extra people. The internship allowed me to learn and build relationships. You usually get hired because of who you know and if you can do the job. The only way to get people to know you and prove yourself is to work for free your first time. You really want to do this any-way because interns are often shown mercy when they make mistakes. If you are being paid and you make many mistakes, you risk being fired and may have difficulty being hired again. As far as Directing and Producing, I acquired these jobs by simply creating them. I want to direct so I write and shoot projects for that purpose. I think of it as creating my own internship. I don't get paid but I get a film to show that I can direct and I get practice to boot. Also, there are many contests and challenges for film-makers these days. I enter as many of these as I can to test my skills against other filmmakers in my area. Plus, many contests offer prize money, exposure, and film equipment as prizes. When you are an established filmmaker, you prove your credi-bility by box office numbers. When you don't have box office numbers to show, you can show awards and accolades you have gotten for your work.

Job search tips, hints, advice, or anecdotes?

If you want to work in the film industry, contact your local film office for a list of upcoming or current productions in your area. Call these companies and ask if they need any help in any department and offer your services for free. You are almost guaranteed to get on set. Then, learn as much as you possibly can and prove to everyone on set that you are a quick learner, a hard worker, and just a cool person

Personal Profile: *Crystle Robertson (continued)*

to have on set (can people tolerate you for 12 hours every day?), have a great attitude and you will be very likely to be hired and paid on the next movie, and the next movie, and the next movie. Also, get out there and shoot! Practice truly makes perfect and the more you get behind that camera the more it becomes a habit and habit becomes skill. Grab some of your filmmaker friends, grab a camera, and go shoot a story to edit. Many times, I approach the Costume Designer's assistant (who really wants to be a Costume Designer one day) and offer them the role of Costume Designer on my movie. Grab the camera assistant and offer them a job as Director of Photography on your film. Many times, they will work with you for free just to get the credit and practice.

Salary

The pay differs from job to job depending on the budget of the production and the type of production it is. For example, a big budget feature pays entry level employees anywhere from $200 to $250 per day while you may only make $75 to $100 per day on a low budget movie. Commercials tend to pay higher day rates, as well as music videos. Once you work for so many days/hours, you may take the option of joining a union. Then, you get guaranteed rates and benefits etc. Directors and Producers usually get around 10 to 20 percent of the budget for the movie/project. So if the project has a budget of $500,000, you can possibly make around $50,000 (and that is a low budget movie).

positions. They tend to be better suited to individuals who possess a bachelor's or other post-secondary degree. However, in lieu of higher education, a proven track record in project development or feature film planning is also highly regarded. As the motion picture industry values on-the-job experience as much as formal education, an internship on the preproduction of a feature film is an invaluable asset.

Entry into this highly lucrative and select group is difficult, but determination and aptitude are recognized by the industry. Since there are many networking opportunities within the various guilds, unions, and societies, an internship may possibly lead to an entry-level position. This is a tremendous incentive for college students to seek out internships. Most university programs in Communications, Mass Media, Film, and Video Production have internship coordinators and intern placement, college programs offer opportunities that are not commonplace outside of the academic setting. In addition, these programs offer networking opportunities for individuals interested in pursuing careers in feature film production. As with internship opportunities, many guilds and societies have apprenticeship programs that are offered to college students. These programs are highly competitive, and the candidates are rigorously scrutinized for their abilities and their suitability for the position.

Fewer employees work during the preproduction phase of feature film production, but they are critical to success and development. Although, as stated above, there are several positions or opportunities for entry-level personnel, it is no assurance of success or longevity in the motion picture industry. A proven record of accomplishment and a list of successful credits are highly valued. The ability to solve problems, handle crises, and affect solutions is another characteristic of successful producers and production personnel.

Production

The production phase of a feature film involves the actual filming or principal photography of a production. It takes careful coordination and organization to prepare for this phase, as it is the most intensive in terms of production personnel, logistics, and cost per production day. On any given production day, numerous below-the-line personnel are employed in their respective disciplines. For example, locations need to be secured, whether they are authentic or studio settings. These costs are much higher on a per diem basis as compared to the preproduction. For this reason, the above-the-line personnel must have every detail and contingency accounted for in the budget. As for the below-the-line personnel, their compensation is based on the number of hours spent working on a production. Regardless of the project outcome—financial failure, or overwhelming success—below-the-line personnel are assured of financial compensation. As the risk is greater for above-the-line personnel, so too are the rewards.

Personal Profile: *Adam Sumner*

Name, title, place of employment, and city/state?

Adam Sumner, Grip/Electric, Freelance, Georgia

Job duties?

I am part of the lighting department. Electrics provide electricity to the set and base camp. They also provide the lights for the scene. Grips shape the light with flags, bounces, and diffusion. Grips also keep an eye on safety issues on set.

What is a typical day like?

A typical day is usually a lot of "hurry up" and "wait." We rush getting lights and equipment in position then tweak everything until it's perfect. Then we wait. Finish the scene and move on to the next one. Repeat as necessary.

How did you obtain your job?

I obtained my job by working hard on low- to no-pay jobs. I kept going until my name started getting passed around the film community. Eventually, I started getting calls for paid gigs.

Job search tips, hints, advice, or anecdotes?

My tip would be, have a good attitude. Networking is a huge part of our community and people remember a good attitude. Go online to websites like mandy.com or Craiglist.com for jobs. These will get your foot in the door.

Salary

My salary differs from job to job. I've been paid as low as $75 a day to $21.75 an hour for 10 weeks of work. About $30,000 to $40,000 is a safe bet if work is steady.

The production process is brief in comparison to the preproduction phase. The time dedicated to production can range from weeks to months to a year or more, depending on the logistics and planning of the motion picture. Below-the-line personnel are contracted to work on the project until completion of the production phase. As this length of time is rather short, it is critical for below-the-line staff to constantly seek out new employment opportunities.

There are several resources that are utilized to maintain employment in the below-the-line or contracted employment realm of motion picture productions. Since guilds, unions, and societies recognize most positions, the networks for these positions are well informed and prolific. To supplement the formal unions, production personnel also have informal networking opportunities available to them. A good example of an informal but essential network contact is the production coordinator. The production coordinator's job is to recruit skilled personnel for an upcoming production. Lastly, most states and major film centers have film boards or offices, which function as a liaison to the industry they serve. These offices are overseen by the state or local government to develop entertainment projects that generate industry and revenue for the communities they serve. They often offer toll-free numbers and websites that list employment opportunities in local film productions. Because the below-the-line production positions are on a temporary employment basis, industry networking is essential. Without a readily available pool of qualified talent and skilled labor, the expansion of production could not be maintained.

Postproduction

The postproduction phase of a feature film immediately follows the principal photography, and includes editing the picture, sound postproduction, special effects, and releasing the film to the public (Konigsberg, 1987). After the completion of the production phase, the production personnel are no longer needed, and postproduction personnel are contracted to complete the film. After principal photography, shots must be organized or sequenced into a coherent production. In addition to editing the images, the sound must be "sweetened," or embellished, to enhance the fictional reality that is filmmaking. The audio enhancement includes dubbing of dialogue; adding natural audio elements, such as ambient noise and natural sounds; and adding the movie score and soundtrack. In coordination with the picture and audio editors, special effects and computer graphics are incorporated frequently to create the illusion of reality. Finally, the film must be distributed for public dissemination, including the theatrical release, DVD, and/or television broadcast. The projected growth cite source in the motion pictures and video industries is attributed to greater demand for video-on-demand, DVDs, and Internet delivery. According to the Bureau of Labor Statistics (2008), the further fragmentation of viewing audiences will create many opportunities to develop films. In particular, the postproduction area will see an increase in employment as computer technologies further influence changes in the production of motion pictures.

Although broad in description, each of the areas just discussed is actually a highly skilled and specific area of the production hierarchy. Depending on the type of film, postproduction may take between 6 months and a year. Often unrecognized for its importance in the production phases, postproduction adds the final touches and enriches the entire production. It is essential to creating a believable and credible project. Again, this phase is carefully coordinated and orchestrated by the above-the-line personnel and must be accounted for in the preproduction process, since it is a costly and expensive part of the movie-making process. With the advent of computer technologies and digital editing and compositing, postproduction is often seen as an area for skilled computer users. However, mastering the machinery is only part of understanding the craft of postproduction. Talented postproduction personnel must be part technician and part creative. They must have the ability to bridge the gap between the technical and the aesthetic. Most great postproduction personnel are paid not for their abilities to push the correct buttons, but for their discerning vision, their ability to listen, or their capacity for design and balance.

Postproduction personnel are also contracted as below-the-line or on a need basis. Their numbers are fewer than what is needed for the production process, but the actual number is based on the needs of the production. As with the other areas of production, entry-level positions are highly competitive. These opportunities are often internships or assistant editor positions. Students in college programs specializing in Communications, Mass Media, Film and Video Production have an advantage here because their schools encourage them to apply for internships. Networking opportunities for these positions are also strong, for the same reasons listed in the previous section on production. As temporary employees, working from job to job, freelancers have evolved a professional infrastructure strong enough to sustain the industry and trade. According to the Bureau of Labor Statistics (2006), the industry will continue to grow by approximately 11 percent, but many positions will open as people leave for more stable employment.

Commercial Production

Commercial production is the development and production of television commercials, public service announcements, and promotional campaigns. The production hierarchy and structure of commercial production differs slightly from that of the feature film industry. In the feature film industry, revenue is secured by a producer to develop a motion picture production. In commercial production, a producer is contracted to serve the needs of an advertising agency or company that wishes to promote a product or service. The outcome of the project is related to production, but indirectly, through product sales or services. Basically, a good film will generate revenue because people will want to see it. For a commercial to be successful, it must generate sales of the product or service it portrays.

This distinguishes the separate categories of personnel with regard to commercial production. It directly impacts the way above-the-line personnel relate to the objectives or purpose of the production. Usually an advertising agency or the promotions department of a company to develop a campaign for a product or service contacts the producer. The strategy and guidelines for the production are clearly outlined, and the above-the-line production personnel calculate a budget and organize the logistics of the request. This is also the time for creative input and revisions to the concept or idea. Quite often, however, the creative development or conceptualization comes from the advertising agency or marketing department of the company. Typically, the above-the-line production personnel are more involved with the execution and completion of the final production. Exhibition or airing of the commercial is also outside of the purview of the production personnel.

The above-the-line personnel function in the same capacity as feature film production but, as stated earlier, their goals and objectives are different. They have a great deal invested in the successful outcome of a production, much like a feature film producer. A successful series or campaign can establish a production company and ensure longevity in the commercial production industry. Since there are companies that solely produce commercial productions, this is another option to consider when seeking employment in the motion picture industry. Entry-level positions are of limited availability, just as they are in feature film production. Internships and volunteering, therefore, are great ways to network and prove merit or value. Film production demands analytical ability, fortitude, and sacrificing personal time, but determined and hard-working individuals can secure positions in the upper echelons in a short time. An entry-level position in the above-the-line area can easily leapfrog over the more intermediate below-the-line production positions.

During commercial production, the below-the-line production personnel are employed in the same manner as in feature film production. Their areas of expertise and skill are required on commercial productions and serve the same function. Below-the-line personnel are contracted on a need basis for the duration of the production. The duration of commercial production shoots (or the production phase) is much shorter than feature film production. Because of this, below-the-line personnel are generously compensated for their work on commercial productions. The unions, guilds, and societies have specific compensation guidelines for this type of production. Due to the temporary employment status of below-the-line production personnel, it is not uncommon for production personnel to work in both feature film and commercial production.

Music Video Production

The music video division of the motion picture industry is comparable to the commercial production area. As with commercial production, music videos are produced with the objective to sell a product. Music video production must focus on the image the company and artist wishes to portray, as well as on selling the music. Great consideration is given to the concept or idea that is presented in the production. In addition to selling music, the video production has great impact on an artist's image and longevity. With the advent of cable and broadcast music video outlets, artists' careers have reaped substantial benefits in terms of increased exposure through music video outlets. As a powerful tool for promotion and artist development, music video outlets rival the marketing potential of the radio industry. In fact, several artists have sustained successful careers solely based on music video exposure, with little or no presence on radio.

Record companies have promotions and artist development representatives who work with artists in creating these promotional videos. Within this department, the record company hires or contracts with a production company to develop a budget, handle production logistics, and hire production personnel. Some creative liberty is given to the production team, but overall control of the creative process is overseen by the record company, artist management, and the artist. As with commercial production, the producer and director of the video relinquish ultimate control to these individuals.

During the preproduction phase, above-the-line personnel present conceptual elements under the guidance or framework presented by the record company, artist management, or artist consent. In some cases, a producer or director is contracted on the merit of past work or stylistic approach. There are varying degrees of creative liberty or control given to the production team depending on this factor. A director with a proven record of accomplishment and extensive portfolio is capable of demanding and receiving greater creative freedom.

The budgets for music videos are directly related to the above-the-line personnel's past work and track record. Although the budgets for music videos have been historically low compared to commercial and feature film production, in certain situations higher budgets are demanded to gain greater artist exposure and to hire the creative talents of recognized production personnel. Spike Lee and Brian DePalma, for example, have directed music videos. Although they are identified first as feature film directors, they have developed creative projects for artists in the music industry.

Music video production also offers up-and-coming producers and directors good opportunities to break into the motion picture industry. With lower-budget projects for unknown artists, record companies often take a calculated risk and produce a video for a nominal investment. Since these projects do not attract A-list talent because of budget constraints, smaller companies and often-independent producers are available. With the advent of inexpensive digital production equipment, production costs have dropped considerably. Using digital video cameras and desktop computer editing, highly imaginative and motivated individuals offer high quality and value to these productions. The greatest challenge for low-budget music video production is not the access to sophisticated equipment, but the need for skilled labor or expertise. It is often difficult to find skilled, below-the-line personnel to work for less money unless there is a lull in production. This affords entry-level personnel opportunities to work on projects with little or no production experience. In both above-the-line and below-the-line categories, music video production can offer entry-level personnel a path to success outside of the traditional production environment or structure.

Below-the-line personnel are contracted on a need basis similar to commercial and feature film production. They work for the length of the project, which can be between one day and one week. Given the brief production phase, music video production is not as lucrative or profitable for below-the-line production personnel. In addition, if work is available on a feature film or commercial production, below-the-line personnel often will not accept work on a music video. This factor affects the amount of production activity. However, as temporary employees, below-the-line personnel will work on a music video, as it is preferable to being unemployed.

Internet video channels, such as YouTube, have enhanced the ability to find greater audiences and given new life to an area of production that has been in decline. After MTV's formative years, during which the majority of its programming was music video based, the transition to reality and episodic shows resulted in less exposure for music videos. YouTube, in particular, has become a popular way for musicians to display their videos, as well as archiving past videos. Lastly, the short narrative style and fast-paced flow of most music videos is a perfect companion to the limited time constraints of YouTube-type Internet video services. Generally, YouTube limits each uploaded video clip to 10 minutes. This time constraint is perfectly suited for most single song music videos. As audiences continue to gravitate to YouTube, young up-and-coming talent has a unique opportunity to produce and distribute their own music videos. YouTube's motto states, "Broadcast Your-self™"—and many novice music video producers are taking advantage of this popular concept.

Production Designations and Descriptions

A list of occupations in the motion picture industry is detailed below. Organized by above-the-line and below-the-line designations, the descriptions are general to the production areas outlined in the chapter.

Above the Line

PRODUCER—Producers develop the project and coordinate the day-to-day operations and logistics of a production. They are responsible for securing the financing and hiring of personnel. The producer oversees all aspects of the project, including the creative, financial, and technical areas, and ensures that the production is completed on time and on schedule. There are different types of producers as they assume various responsibilities in the coordination and production of a motion picture. Some designations in this occupation include Executive Producer, Associate Producer, Line Producer, and Producer Manager.

DIRECTOR—The director oversees the overall creative aspects of a production and is responsible for interpreting the written script and thematic vision into a motion picture. This person interacts with all technical and creative personnel on a production under the financial and scheduling supervision of the producer.

PRODUCTION DESIGNER—The production designer oversees the look of the setting and environments in the motion picture. The production designer also coordinates the activities of the art department.

ASSISTANT DIRECTOR—The assistant director assists the producer in handling logistical details related to the production of a motion picture. The assistant director is an intermediate between the director, producer, and production personnel, and reports to the producer.

WRITER—The writer, also known as the screenwriter, develops an idea or concept and writes the screenplay or script for the motion picture production. If the idea or story is taken from an existing literary work, it is referred to as an adaptation. The writer works closely with the producer and director to develop the project for a visual medium, as opposed to words to be read on a page. Given this consideration, a script will usually go through several revisions before it is ready for the production phase.

It is also likely that more than one writer will work on any given production. In the development phase, one writer will prepare the initial script. In subsequent revisions, other writers work under the supervision and guidance of the director and producer. By the completion of the project, the script has been refined or honed by several writers, and the final script is transformed under the creative guidance or vision of the director.

Below the Line

CINEMATOGRAPHER—The cinematographer, or DP (Director of Photography), works under the direct supervision of the director. It is the cinematographer's responsibility to translate the director's vision into photographic or electronic images. Framing each image, the use of light and color, camera movement, and coordination of the camera personnel are all responsibilities of the cinematographer.

Within the camera crew, there are, in order of importance, first and second camera assistants, camera operators, gaffers, and electricians. Each occupation has its specific responsibilities and tasks:

- CAMERA ASSISTANTS are responsible for the assembly, loading, and maintenance of the camera. Generally, there is a first and second camera assistant assigned to a project.
- CAMERA OPERATORS are in control of the camera during filming or taping.
- GAFFERS (key) are electricians responsible for the placement and functionality of the lighting. Working under the supervision of the cinematographer, the gaffer performs the logistics of lighting the shot.
- ELECTRICIANS are supervised by the gaffer and assist in the process of lighting for the camera.
- GRIP DEPARTMENT (key, dolly, and grip) Grips are responsible for a variety of tasks on the set. They transport and set up lighting, scenery, props, and the dolly. The KEY grip supervises all of the other stagehands and grips. The DOLLY grip lays the dolly track and is responsible for pushing the dolly while executing camera movement. The term GRIP is the general designation for anyone who carries something.

SOUND MIXER—The sound mixer, or recordist, is responsible for capturing production audio for the project. It is the mixer's responsibility to determine the best approach and technique to improve or alter the sound quality.

BOOM OPERATOR—The boom operator works in conjunction with the sound mixer to place the microphone on axis or in a position that best captures the dialogue, ambience, or action of the shot.

ART DIRECTOR—The art director works with the production designer and is responsible for the environment or setting of the production. Sets, locations, and exteriors are dressed or modified to create the proper mood or tone of the project. These modifications include the color scheme, furniture, props, and fixtures. The art director works under the supervision of the producer, director, and the production designer.

Within the art department, there are many diverse and specific positions. These occupations include set designers, model makers, carpenters, painters, laborers, and set decorators. The hierarchy in these occupations is as follows: production designer, art director, set decorator, lead scenic, construction coordinator, and lead man.

COSTUME DESIGNER—The costume designer is responsible for the design and creation of the wardrobe for the actors to reflect the proper ambiance and period of the film. Other occupations within the costume area include costume supervisor, costumer, and seamstress or tailor.

MAKEUP ARTIST—The makeup artist applies makeup to the performers, which aids in the transformation of the actors into the characters they portray. Another occupation in the area of makeup is HAIRSTYLIST.

ACTOR—The actor portrays a character and interprets character roles in the production of motion pictures. Acting is one of the most competitive and highly selective occupations in the motion picture industry, and it is also one of the most highly sought after. Although only a small group of actors attain recognition and success, there are many actors who fill the smaller support roles known as walk ons or extras. Typically, the producer and director select actors by the process of audition.

AGENT—Most actors are represented by a facilitator, who is usually contacted by the producer, or casting director, and arranges for the actor to audition for a role in the production.

CASTING DIRECTOR—It is the casting director's responsibility to contact agents and coordinate the audition process.

LOCATION MANAGER—The location manager scouts locations and makes the logistical arrangements to shoot in specific places.

EDITOR—The editor selects the best shots and performances and assembles the material in a logical sequence. Depending on the script or concept of the production, the editor is given considerable creative liberty to discern what has creative value. While not fully autonomous, an editor is valued for his or her unique ability to approach the material from a fresh perspective. Although the producer and often the director oversee the creative process, it is the responsibility of the editor to maintain the director's vision for the story.

Within the editorial staff, there is a support occupation in the process of post-production, referred to as an ASSISTANT EDITOR.

AUDIO EDITOR or ENGINEER—During the production process, the audio editor or engineer supervises the postproduction audio processes. These processes include automatic dialogue replacement (ADR), Foley, scoring, insertion of soundtrack, and the final mixdown of the entire audio sequence. Often one of the most overlooked areas of motion picture production, the audio postproduction process is an invaluable part of the production.

Within the audio postproduction area, there are several support occupations coordinated by the producer. These audio occupations include assistant editors, dubbing editors, Foley artists, musicians, composers, and studio engineers.

MULTIMEDIA ARTIST and ANIMATOR—As computer and digital technologies have become essential tools in the process of creating motion pictures, the demand for skilled computer technicians and artists has increased. Multimedia artists and animators are often employed throughout the production and postproduction processes. While the demand for multimedia artists is great, it is also dependent on the concept or need of the production.

PRODUCTION ASSISTANT—Support occupations are greatly needed in all phases of the production process. Within every area and department, there is a need for production assistants. These entry-level positions support and assist production personnel in every capacity. The variety of tasks can range from moving property, running errands, assisting with extras, carrying equipment, or assisting with any need not performed by the other skilled occupations. As utility personnel, production assistants are required to work long hours and are expected to perform onerous tasks. However, production assistant occupations are capable of gaining valuable on-the-job experience that results in opportunities for advancement. According to the Kodak Essential Reference Guide for Filmmakers (2006), occupation designations vary from film to film. Depending on the budget and complexity of the script, crew size can vary greatly. A large-budget feature film may potentially employ hundreds of people, while a low-budget feature may have just a dozen key positions.

Production Occupations for Motion Pictures	
Preproduction	Producer Director Assistant Director Writer Production Designer Art Director Set Designer Lead Man Set Dresser Carpenter Costume Designer Casting Director
Production	Director Assistant Director Script Supervisor Cinematographer Gaffer Best Boy Camera Crew Grips Dolly Grip Location Manager Makeup Sound Mixer Boom Operator Actor Stand-in
Postproduction	Editor Audio Engineer Multimedia Artist or Animator
All Phases	Production Assistant

Conclusion

The occupations described in this chapter are directly related to the creative and technical occupations in the motion picture industries. In addition to these areas, there are many lateral or related positions in this multi-faceted industry. According to occupational statistics provided by the U.S. Bureau of Labor Statistics (2006), "professionals and related workers account for about 3 in 10 salaried jobs in the industry." Many of these related occupations are within the service industry.

In the professional occupations of the motion picture industry, there are management, business and financial occupations involving studio management, marketing and distribution, accounting and auditing, law, and other business related activities. These professions, while not directly related to the production process of motion pictures, are essential to the industry. As opposed to the production driven area of the motion pictures industry, the professional areas handle the day-to-day operations and business infrastructure that finance and maintain production. One of the many benefits provided by management is the ability to sustain the industry by means of checks and balances. As with any business endeavor, profits must sustain an operation. The motion picture industry is a careful balance of hits and misses offset by these financial entities. Without the careful coordination and oversight of finances, the industry could not exist.

In the service and related industries, there are occupations in food services, clerical and secretarial, retail sales, manufacturing and warehousing, shipping and receiving, as well as janitorial and maintenance. These support occupations are as necessary as any other area in the industry. Much like the professional occupations, these services are often unrecognized. While formal education or knowledge of the motion picture industry is not requisite, these occupations can lead to opportunities in other areas of the industry.

As a final note, the qualities and traits preferred in the motion picture industry are not unique. Any determined and motivated individual is capable of finding success in the industry. It is a highly competitive and complex industry that survives on the creative and technical abilities of the various production entities. Additionally, the industry will continue to sustain growth as the need for entertainment and promotional programming continues to expand.

REFERENCES

Bernstein, Steven. *The Technique of Film Production*, Second Edition. Focal Press, 1997.

The Essential Reference Guide for Filmmakers, Kodak Publishing, 2006.

Konigsberg, Ira. *The Complete Film Dictionary*, Meridian, 1987.

U.S. Bureau of Labor Statistics Office of Occupational Statistics and Employment Projections, Career Guide to Industries: Broadcasting, 2006 <www.bls.gov/oco/cg>.

7 New Media

The Growth of New Media

The term New Media refers to use of computers for multimedia production and project development. It also refers to the change in traditional models and roles involving media production as the convergence of technologies continues to affect the way media is produced and delivered. As the production process adapts to digital technologies and increasing reliance on the use of computers, traditional occupations will be transformed and shaped by new processes. Digital production equipment is smaller, cheaper, easier to use, and creates media at a level of sophistication exceeding viewer and customer expectations. In addition, it has consolidated media markets, redefined industries, and shifted occupational prospects and opportunities. As there will be an increase in media related opportunities, the majority of those positions will be in New Media. According to the *Occupational Outlook Handbook* (2008–2009), occupations involving computer skills will continue to see the greatest growth.

New Media crosses over into all areas of media production. It has great influence on the traditional business models of radio, television, motion pictures, print and broadcast journalism, the music industry, advertising, and public relations. New Media is also an integral part of media production processes. Journalists now use satellite phones and the Internet for newsgathering and dissemination. Broadcast operations use automated systems on computer servers instead of traditional tape-based, manually controlled programming. Radio stations are also computer automated, relying heavily on syndicated programming delivered by satellite or computer network. The motion picture industry now edits most feature films on digital, non-linear, computer-based systems. These same films are distributed on interactive DVDs. Network television generates an increasing amount of revenue by distributing and packaging entire seasons of television shows on DVD and online services such as iTunes, Amazon, and Hulu. The music industry has been contending with new delivery systems of music since the MP3 revolutionized the dissemination of produced music.

The transition to New Media is directly related to the transition from analog to digital technologies in the media industries. The commonality is the use of computers across all areas. With the cost of computers declining, inexpensive access to sophisticated software, and a robust network infrastructure, the transformation not only affects media industries, but also media consumers. Our society's media choices have been greatly enriched by the digital revolution and New Media. Gone are the days of limited access to television, radio, landline telephones, and computer media. It is now commonplace to have a variety of sophisticated media outlets within every home. Cable and satellite television offer hundreds of channels of video programming. Broadcast radio now offers many syndicated programming options. Satellite radio offers hundreds of channels of digital quality audio programming.

Most home computers have access to broadband Internet and the World Wide Web. The Internet alone is a seemingly inexhaustible source of news, entertainment, and information. With the advent of IPTV and broadband delivery systems, there will be an increase in content delivery via computer networks. For example, Netflix offers a set-top box that will provide access to movies over high-speed Internet connections. (Netflix built its service providing next-day shipping to customers from its DVD library.) The new service offered by Netflix provides instant access to its collection using video streaming. According to Netflix (2008), 10 million movies and TV episodes have been viewed so far. As media providers continue to find new means of delivering content to consumers, there will be an increase in demand for media. According to Adams Media Research (2008), Internet downloads will top $4 billion by the year 2011. Consumption will drive both the conversion of archive materials and the production of new entertainment.

To fully explain New Media and its occupational outlook, a comparison of tradition media and New Media in their related industries is necessary

Television

Changes in the Industry

In recent years, occupations in television and broadcasting have been in transition because of consolidation within the industry. With the recent Federal Communications Commission (FCC) changes to ownership restrictions and market limitations, many of the larger media companies have purchased a growing number of local stations, increasing their presence in markets throughout the country. This consolidation has limited and restricted local television operations and local news. These larger holding companies have not found it cost effective to produce local news and entertainment shows. Local news was a traditional fixture of local television scheduling, but as costs have increased and television audiences have gravitated to New Media areas, syndicated television programs have become a cost effective option. Therefore, occupations in these markets have evolved to meet these changes, reducing the number of traditional production occupations, but increasing opportunities in sales, promotion, and New-Media production. Individuals who have been trained in New Media will have a distinct advantage in securing future employment in the changing landscape of television broadcasting.

In addition to media consolidation, changes in technology and media convergence have also greatly affected the operations and occupational outlook in these industries. The DTV conversion mandated by the FCC to take effect in February of 2009 has hastened the change from traditional production techniques to New-Media technologies. The New-Media revolution has changed the operations of television production, broadcast delivery systems, newsgathering, and promotions within the television industry. As television continues to lose portions of its audience to Internet usage, the television industry will change even further. Opportunities in traditional television occupations will decline.

Distribution (Master Control)

A television signal is delivered over the broadcast airwaves, through coaxial cable, or via digital satellite transmissions. All three of these sources have one thing in common; they originate at a source called the head end. At this point of origin, an operator who coordinates these various operations controls the programming, advertisements, and graphic insertions. Traditionally, the programs and advertisements were placed on analog tape sources and played when needed. In this master control environment, the operator sat at a control board or panel that remotely operated a bank of videotape machines that contained the broadcast programs. In addition to taped programming, the master control operator also fed the signal that contained live programs, such as the local news or sporting events, while inserting taped commercial and promotional productions.

New Media is now transforming this traditional method of disseminating or broadcasting television signals. Although the airwaves, coaxial cable, and satellite transmissions are still being utilized for delivery, computers have increasingly automated master control environments. In addition to automation, computers called video servers, which store and play video programs on demand, are replacing analog tape systems. These digitally based systems are more convenient and efficient since they do not require multiple mechanical machines nor do they require rewinding, fast-forwarding, and tape-based systems that break down or wear out after multiple uses.

Promotions

Many television stations have promotions departments, which manage the station's public image. These departments produce short video clips highlighting community relations, programming, news, and a host of other benefits. Traditionally, production was performed on analog media equipment employing techniques that were compatible with single camera, film style production. Stations now must maintain a presence on the Internet, and the promotional productions have become far savvier, including multimedia components and graphics.

The change in occupations in promotions is reflected by current job descriptions. In addition to the traditional skills of writing and creative thinking, candidates for employment must have technical and computer abilities in multimedia and digital editing applications. As with most departments within the television hierarchy, computers are playing a greater role in day-to-day operations.

News

The news production workplace has been changing rapidly because of the increasing use of computers and media convergence. Because news production is of the few areas in the production environment that is still executed live, the workflow and orchestration of the program must be highly efficient and meticulously organized. Coincidentally, the benefits of digital media and computer operations are that they are integrated, fast, efficient, and cost effective. These qualities have quickly changed the industry and standards for news production in the field and studio.

Field production, or electronic newsgathering (ENG) footage, is shot on video. The information is edited into a package to be "rolled" into the live newscast. Traditionally this process involved shooting on analog video systems and before

Personal Profile: *Kate Gelsthorpe*

Name, job title, place of employment, and city/state

Kate Spencer Gelsthorpe, Web Content Producer, WSB-TV, Atlanta, Georgia

Job duties

I am responsible for all things wsbtv.com. My main objectives are to keep our site constantly updated with the news of the day and to achieve as many page views as possible. I write news stories exclusively for the site, I repurpose scripts from our shows for the site, I upload videos, web exclusive elements (PDFs, Warrants, Video extras), create slideshows, quizzes, and surveys. My station has an agreement with CNN.com and I work with them as well to create local and regional stories that they use on their site. I am responsible for creating special web pages to promote local programming shows. I work closely with our sales department to come up with ideas for our clients that we can incorporate on the site.

What is a typical day like?

I work 10 a.m. to 7 p.m., Monday through Friday. A typical day for me—it's just constant! I hit the ground running and don't stop until I leave! First thing is I upload 5 new videos and add 5 new headlines to the homepage. I update the Entertainment, Health, Pets pages. I look through our assign file and get an idea of what the news department will be covering for the noon show. The noon lunch hour is our most highly trafficked time so that's when I'm slammed with updates— writing new stories, repurposing scripts from the show. We have a news meeting at 2 p.m. to go over what we'll be covering in the 5 & 6 o'clock shows. I completely redo the homepage (all new main stories, headlines, and videos) during the 5 o'clock hour. And in the middle of all of that, I meet with sales about ideas, pitch stories to CNN, work closely with our assignment desk to get warrants, mug shots.

How did you obtain your job?

I got a part-time production assistant job with WSB right out of school because a college classmate of mine was interning here and got me an interview. From there, I trained in the graphics department, which turned into a full-time job for me. While working full-time in graphics, I worked a 6th day as a news writer because that was where my interest was. That cross training helped me gain the opportunity to produce a couple of shows. Because of my graphics and news writing experience, the head of the web department approached me about the job and now I've been doing web for three years.

Job search tips, hints, advice, or anecdotes

My advice would be to be interested in learning as much as possible—even if you're not in the exact job you want right away! Take that experience and show hard work, determination and a lot of interest—and people will notice and it can turn into something you do want. You have to put in your time, but for me, it was worth it. Keep in touch with classmates and former co-workers—they were/have been my best contacts through the years.

Salary

$47,000 to $51,000

that, on film, eventually edited on a linear video editing system for the final package. This package was placed on tape, inserted into a video tape deck, and literally rolled into the newscast when cued by the live director. This system or workflow required careful orchestration and meticulous detail on the part of the tape operator, director, package editor, and any other personnel involved in the process.

With the advent of computer editing and digital technologies, the same footage may now be shot on digital video cameras onto disk or card-based recorders. The footage is immediately imported into a computer system for non-linear digital editing, and the completed package can then be exported into a video file for placement onto a video server. The server is integrated into the production environment and can be played back instantaneously by the technical director, who used the production switcher to select the source. This digital workflow is far more efficient and less prone to human error or failure. In addition, the process involves fewer personnel and less transportation because of file sharing (versus traditional mail or hand delivery).

Within the studio environment, robotic cameras have now taken the place of human operators. Teleprompters are no longer hard copy, paper-based systems; they are computerized. The tape-based system of rolling in packages has been replaced by computer server based systems that play a package without the assistance of human tape operators. The term used to describe this new type of automation and reliance on computers is referred to as workflow. As the workflow becomes more efficient and streamlined, the dependency on people is reduced. However, while the number of occupations in the area of television news is in decline, there is an increasing demand for personnel skilled in New Media, computer skills, and digital technologies.

Within the Production

Within the television production area, the mission of the Promotions department is to produce programming, commercials, or any production not related to the news or promotional operations of the station. Production departments vary in size, depending on the market and need for production in a specific geographic area. Some production departments are in great demand, while others are not necessary due to outside production companies or the demands of the community. Regardless of the production output, the demand for greater sophistication in programming and commercials compels production departments to rely on new technologies and multimedia. Regarding commercial and motion picture production, the techniques and skills are similar, but have been evolving due to the changes in technology and media convergence.

Specific changes in technology and an increasing reliance on computers have affected the process of production. In editing video for television and broadcasting, tape-based analog video systems were traditionally utilized for production and dissemination. Many were component systems requiring expensive separate and specific electronic equipment to perform one function. Traditional tape-to-tape editing required individual machines, edit controllers, time-based correctors, video distribution amplifiers, and numerous other devices to perform linear tape editing. With the advent of digital computer-based, nonlinear editing, this expensive equipment has been replaced by software. This equipment requires much less money, and a smaller staff, to operate.

In television production, there is greater demand for sophistication regarding graphics and visual effects. Gone are the days of talking head testimonials and slow-paced narrative productions. The pacing and visual sophistication of television commercials and programs demands the use of computer graphics, multimedia applications, and motion effects. This new area of media production generates job opportunities for persons skilled in New Media, who have the creative vision and ability to innovate and dazzle audiences. As New Media continues to change the television industry, the occupational outlook will transform from traditional production occupations to occupations with expertise in New Media.

Radio

Increasing consolidation and media convergence has also taken its toll on traditional occupations in the radio industry. On-air talent occupations are expected to continue its decline in occupational outlook. With new technologies and satellite radio, the traditional business model for radio is being transformed and streamlined. Consolidation is limiting local ownership and programming further reducing occupations in radio. It also increases reliance on syndicated programming, which results in fewer opportunities for radio talent. New technologies offer alternatives to radio programming in the form of satellite radio, podcasting, and personal media devices. Moreover, digital technologies have simplified the production equipment and techniques utilized in the production of radio, reducing the need for technical occupations in the industry. As with the television industry, New Media is contributing to the transformation of the occupational outlook in the radio industry.

Personal Profile: *Jason Tyler*

Name, title, place of employment, and city/state?
Jason Tyler, Media Manager, Crawford Communications, Inc., Atlanta, Georgia

Job duties?
Responsible for quality control of all content that will originate from Master Control, train and manage a staff of eight operators for Network Origination and QC, and ensure that specified technical network procedures are being satisfied.

What is a typical day like?
Arrive at 7 a.m. to obtain shift reports from the previous evening to troubleshoot any problems, Check all traffic logs for any missing materials, obtain schedules for equipment maintenance from Broadcast Engineering, meet with Network Managers for any issues they may have with equipment or content, instruct staff on any special assignments outside of normal operations, update Director of Network Operations on previous night's events, and update Network Supervisor at the end of the day.

How did you obtain your job?
I started as a Master Control Operator for Crawford Communications in 2001. I made a point of learning all broadcast platforms that were utilized at Crawford Communications. I was promoted to a Network Manager position in 2003. When a new multi-channel system was brought in for Network Operations, I was assigned with the task of learning the new operating platform and instructing others. I now

Personal Profile: *Jason Tyler (continued)*

manage media and staff across four broadcast platforms originating over 35 standard-definition channels and two high-definition channels.

Job search tips, hints, advice, or anecdotes?

Learn more than just the job you are assigned: The more of an asset you are to your company, the more opportunities you will have to advance. Negative attitudes and talk are the fastest way to be removed from your job.

What is your salary or salary range?

The salary for this job varies by market and company size, but $40K to $60K seems to be the range I have seen with other companies.

Radio Programming

As previously stated, there has been considerable consolidation within the radio industry. Local ownership has declined as large media corporations have purchased radio stations because of changes in the FCC regulations governing broadcast ownership. Companies like Clear Channel have transformed the local radio market by consolidating several media outlets under one company or owner. Consolidating radio with other forms of media advertising, Clear Channel can offer a variety of media outlets for advertisers and the markets they serve. This model has been cost effective, and has streamlined the industry. As a result, traditional occupations in radio have declined.

Because of this consolidation, the larger media companies have reduced on-air talent or announcers locally. It is cost effective to have on-air talent in a few markets produce local inserts for several stations or markets, rather than employing talent at every station. In addition to local inserts and breaks, syndicated programming is a cost-effective innovation. New Media and digital technologies have simplified and facilitated this process. With digital recording and computer automation systems, large media companies have the technical means to consolidate on-air production, thus decreasing the operating costs. This allows for conformity and consistent professional output, without the redundancy of multiple production facilities to maintain and staff. The use of digital technologies has facilitated consolidation, which is now the standard in the radio industry.

Motion Pictures

The primary occupations in New Media within the motion picture industry are multimedia artists and animators. With computers and digital technologies, the creation of fictional settings, environments, and special effects has been greatly enhanced by multimedia and animation applications. Companies like Industrial Light and Magic and Digital Domain have revolutionized special effects in film production. These sophisticated effects and techniques have become commonplace in the production of motion pictures. In addition, audiences have higher expectations and a more sophisticated eye for effects in movies and popular entertainment. Even the most basic character driven narratives utilize digital effects and techniques. Whether it is to enhance period pieces, create fictional environments, or simulate natural disasters, the seamless integration of special effects is now part of the production environment.

As the Occupational Outlook (2008) for the motion picture industry states, there will be growth in the demand for multimedia artists and animators. The greater dependency on computers for the creation of motion pictures has consequently increased the demand for personnel skilled in computer technologies and applications. As with virtually all other areas of media production, the motion picture industry is in transition from occupations that require traditional skills within the industry to occupations requiring skill in New Media and digital technologies.

Editing

Digital technologies have transformed the process of editing film for motion pictures. They have also altered the role of the editor. In the past, film editing was a mechanical, "hands-on" process involving physically cutting a strip of film and taping the shots into coherent sequences. As computers and digital technologies have become more powerful and affordable, it is now feasible to digitize the raw footage and edit the film on a computer. In addition to being efficient and cost effective, the process is nondestructive and it establishes a digital workflow that is compatible with other digital postproduction processes and effects.

One of the innovations in this digital workflow is the use of digital intermediates. In this digital area of postproduction, often referred to as electronic post, the edited project is electronically scanned, so that a variety of color correction and visual effects can be incorporated into the finished production. This process has been popular with higher budget productions, but only recently become affordable and prevalent in moderate- to lower-budget productions. With this increase in digital intermediate services, the occupational outlook has paralleled the increase in the industry. In addition to the increase in occupational opportunities, many traditional postproduction industries have adapted their business model and product development in these areas. In particular, Kodak and Technicolor now offer digital intermediate services and facilities. With this major shift in the production environment, skills in New Media and digital technologies will become valuable assets when seeking employment in the motion picture industry.

Distribution

Analogous to digital workflow is DVD production. In recent years, DVD sales and rentals have overtaken the home consumer market. Superior to the analog VHS format, this digital format offers better quality and supplemental production materials. In addition to the feature presentation, DVD releases offer a variety of materials, including behind-the-scenes footage, interviews, and director commentary. This area of postproduction has spawned an increase in occupational opportunities in multimedia and New Media. An additional benefit to traditional production occupations is the growing need for production personnel to create the supplemental productions now standard on DVD releases.

The sale of DVDs, particularly of television series, has increased revenues and profitability in the entertainment industry. As ticket sales to theatrical releases decline, the growth in DVD sales is sustaining the industry. Marketed at a lower cost than the traditional VHS release, DVDs appeal to consumers who wish to buy movies instead of renting them. In the past, the audiences of television series were

Personal Profile: *Thomas Nay*

Name, title, place of employment, and city/state?

Thomas Nay, Corporate Internet Content Director, Black Crow Media Group, Daytona Beach, Florida

Job duties?

I assist our different radio station websites in finding compelling content for their individual station websites. I also keep an eye on developing technologies and trends in the media industry to better understand our needs. Another aspect of my job is developing our online media properties. I measure and report our online growth and progress.

What is a typical day like?

My day starts out typically catching up on my emails and prioritizing what needs to be taken care of. I typically have benchmarks in specific projects that I work on daily. I have weekly meetings that I attend and discuss upcoming projects. One of the great things about my job is that it is constantly evolving and growing. I take a look at our analytics and try to measure how content is being used on our websites. I spend time speaking with different types of vendors to take a look at what products they have to offer for our websites.

How did you obtain your job?

I had been working for this particular company for almost 4-and-a-half years and had just graduated from college. I was looking for some other opportunities. Basically, I made mention to the owner of the company that I enjoyed working with our websites. A week or two later they asked me if I'd be interested in a position with the entire company focusing on the content provided by our station websites. A handful of discussions later I was moving to Daytona Beach. Having some background in working with the web helped out a lot as well. I felt like this was a great opportunity to learn and expand my knowledge. The radio industry is in the process of evolving towards digital media, and this is a great time to get involved in this growing part of the business.

Do you have any job search tips, hints, advice, or anecdotes?

When it comes to job search I must say that you have to network. Networking is absolutely essential in this industry because you never know where you will end up. Networking is that one thing that can almost open any door or close every door you find. Keep your eyes open as well. If you spent most of your time in college behind a camera doesn't mean you have to go work for a television station or network. The way the industry is headed all forms of media are utilizing video on the web. Media is changing, in the way it's produced and the way it's consumed over the next few years we will continue to watch all barriers to entry fall. Now is the time to look toward the future and be flexible. Break out of the traditional thinking of television, radio, and newspapers—the Internet replaces all of them. Another thing to remember is to listen and learn! Especially early in your career.

What is your salary or salary range?

Internet content directors in media can make anywhere from $30,000 in the smaller places to upwards of $100,000 in large markets. The salaries differ greatly between mediums, markets, and size of the company you are working for.

limited by the number of times a show was broadcast, but subsequent marketing of the series via DVD has offered a new revenue stream for the producers. Shows like *Seinfeld, Friends*, and *The Sopranos* have become best sellers in the DVD market. This residual benefit has increased profitability in the entertainment industry, therefore creating more opportunities for employment.

Portable and Wireless Technologies

iPods

With the introduction of Apple's iPod, consumers embraced portable digital audio players, greatly affecting how consumers access music, radio programs, and news. Although not the first player on the market, iPod's stylish shape and ease of use solidified its position in the consumer electronics market. Utilizing the MP3 and MPEG4 formats, iPod and other portable digital audio players have greatly affected traditional methods of dissemination and delivery of audio content. Beginning with Napster and peer-to-peer file sharing, the MP3 format, in particular, signaled a change in the media landscape for the music and radio industries.

With increasing computer processing and network infrastructure, the ease and quality of reproducing audio content facilitated changes in these industries. Initially utilized for illegal downloading and sharing of pirated music, the MP3 market has transformed itself into a legal and prolific market for music, news, and radio programs. It has changed traditional methods of distribution, such as through record stores and local radio. Instead of purchasing a compact disc at the local record store, consumers can log on to Amazon, Napster, or Apple's iTunes to get the latest releases from their favorite artist. This is done at a nominal cost, and reduces the need for inventory, physical brick-and-mortar stores, and wholesalers.

Apple's latest innovation in the portable media player market is the ability to store and play videos, greatly expands the realm of possibilities for the portable media player market. Initially devised as a device to store and play personal music files, the iPod has evolved to become a multiuse media device that plays music, syndicated radio programs, news programs, and now video. This method of delivery, referred to as Podcasting, is a fast growing area of New Media and is expanding occupational opportunities in the production of content for portable media. Podcasting is made possible through the Internet, which allows users either to subscribe or purchase content, usually in the form of an MP3 file. Much like the innovation of weblogs, Podcasting allows individuals, as well as traditional media producers, to distribute content direct to the consumer. This innovation has offered greater access to content at a manageable cost. Lower distribution costs have also allowed independent media producers to circumvent the traditional media distributors or gatekeepers due to the lower cost for distribution. In addition to Apple's iPod, the iPhone has set the standard as an all-in-one personal media device. The iPhone epitomizes the convergence of media, and has been tremendously successful at tapping into the public's demand for mobile communication and portable media content.

RSS

RSS is utilized for web syndication. It is used by news websites, weblogs, and a host of other commercial and individual informational websites. RSS is an acronym for Rich Site Summary or Really Simple Syndication, and creates a relationship between the information provider and the receiver or consumer. The user subscribes to an RSS service, and is regularly updated or provided content from the syndication source. For multimedia, RSS can deliver audio and video media files, specifically MP3 file types, or Podcasting. Initially used to relay text messages, RSS has expanded, relaying headlines, sports scores, and short summary stories. RSS will become an even more viable form of entertainment, news, and promotion for consumers as the use of portable media devices like the iPod increases. RSS feeds are now being utilized to deliver radio programming to individual listeners. As part of Podcasting, individuals receive programs directly to a portable media device, bypassing any traditional means of broadcast or distribution. As this new area of media continues to expand, experts in technology and New Media will see an increase in occupational outlook.

Cellular Phones

Another growing area of convergent media is the use of wireless technologies. In particular, cellular phones are expanding the media offerings for consumers. Cellular phones are no longer solely used for person-to-person communication. In addition to interpersonal communication, cell phones offer many uses to the consumer including digital photography, video recording, and MP3 players. In conjunction with RSS and downloadable services like Napster and iTunes, cellular phones are becoming comparable to the iPod and MP3 players. One of the services that have recently come to the forefront of the media world is the use of musical ringtones. Ringtones are songs that replace the traditional phone ringer. In the summer of 2005, a phone ringtone topped the charts on the British music charts for the first time. Companies typically charge $1.00 to $4.00 for use of a pop song as a ringtone. Due to the popularity of this service, music charts, which are comparable to the Billboard music charts utilized by the music industry, have been devised to rank ringtone sales.

Apple's iPhone is changing the way consumers utilize cellular phones. As an all-in-one media device, the iPhone is a cell phone with the capabilities of an iPod and Wi-Fi Internet access and functionality. The iPhone and its competitors, the Blackberry and the Treo, offer far more features than traditional cellular phones. They provide Internet access and email with sophisticated operating systems similar to those designed for personal computers. The iPhone, in particular, appeals to popular culture by offering the style, interface, and functionality of an iPod, with enhanced telephone and Wi-Fi capabilities. The latest version of the iPhone is built on the 3G wireless standard, which allows for faster access to email, the Internet, and downloadable materials. These materials include applications (referred to as apps), such as video games, business tools, and GPS (Global Positioning System). The iPhone also offers access to Apple's iTunes with its collection of songs, movies, and television shows. This vast collection of media is available to iPhone users for a fee for each item selected.

These innovations in the wireless market are compelling media content producers to find niche markets and audiences. As the infrastructure and devices become cheaper and more readily available, content production will need to keep up with the demand. As our society becomes more mobile and moves away from traditional sources of media, the demand for wireless services, information, and entertainment will further erode traditional occupations in media production.

Streaming Technologies

With the proliferation of Internet media and increasing broadband access to the Internet, the demand for rich media content is increasing occupational prospects for personnel skilled in New Media and digital technologies. As the cost of computer processing speed, storage, and bandwidth continues to decrease, the Internet will further transform how consumers utilize online media. As a facilitator of media convergence, Internet media content will no longer be solely text and graphic-based sources of information, advertising, and entertainment. Services such as YouTube and Hulu have made video on the Internet commonplace. The average Internet user has developed an expectation of ever-more-sophisticated Internet content. Traditional dissemination of computer-based media utilizes text, pictures, and graphics. Recent developments in computer technologies have made it possible to incorporate sophisticated animation, audio, and video as part of a site's content. In particular, Macromedia's Flash video software has revolutionized the standard for creating and delivering web animation and embedded video content.

The innovations and capabilities of streaming technologies have expanded the computer media experience, and offer greater potential for further convergence of media sources. Streaming media is described as broadcasting, but differs from traditional forms of television and radio broadcasting. A fundamental difference is the interactivity and on-demand capabilities of web-based streaming. Additionally, on-demand streaming allows the audience to view a clip or program at their discretion, with the ability to pause or replay the media on demand.

The television industry, including cable and broadcast outlets, will experience declines in audience share as consumers turn to the Internet for video programming and episodic entertainment. Many producers are embracing this form of delivery, and offer content on pay sites such as Apple's iTunes or on free services such as Hulu. Tom Green, of the influential *Tom Green Show* on MTV, has returned to the Internet as the primary vehicle for disseminating his content. Green, initially known for his embedded audio clips and website, became one of MTV's most popular celebrities. His current site, TomGreen.com, offers live and archived content via streaming technology. Without the restraints of traditional FCC broadcast guidelines, Green's irreverent content and style reach his audience unfettered, and Green serves as a model for Internet broadcasting.

The radio industry is also experiencing a decline in audience to streaming content, podcasting, and the portable media players previously described. Lastly, the music industry has seen declines in revenue as distribution has been greatly affected by the technologies related to New Media and their corresponding outlets for dissemination. Although the demand for content remains constant, traditional outlets for media are experiencing a decline in audience share. To offset this decline, many traditional industries have adapted New-Media technologies and streaming capabilities to achieve greater access to markets. As audiences move to new forms of distribution and dissemination utilizing New-Media devices, wireless technologies, and the Internet, occupational prospects will increase in these areas.

Video Games

Video games have been evolving for the past 35 years. Video gaming has enjoyed great success and longevity as the popularity of interactive games has increased with advances in New-Media technologies. The first mass-marketed video game,

"Pong," was incredibly popular, but pales in comparison to the sophistication and interactive nature of today's video game offerings. As software developers create more realistic and lifelike games, the audience for gaming will continue to thrive and flourish. Previously considered a market for teenage boys, the video game market is expanding and maturing. In recent years, the industry has seen an increase in women playing games. In fact, women outnumber men in playing web-based computer games. "More recent games such as *The Sims* were huge crossover successes that attracted many women who had never played games before," according to Henry Jenkins (2005), a professor at MIT and Co-Director of the MIT Comparative Media Studies Program.

The reoccurring notion of convergent media is mirrored by the increasing popularity and diversification of video games across platforms. With the advent of personal computers in homes, video games became more readily available. As audiences gravitated to computers, companies developed more sophisticated and powerful stand-alone units that rival the processing power of personal computers. With the development of the Sony PlayStation 3, the Nintendo Wii, and the Microsoft Xbox 360, consumers can buy high-powered game consoles without the high cost and technical prowess necessary to use personal computers. Similarly, these console systems are capable of Internet connectivity, allowing for greater access to gaming networks and user groups. These virtual communities are decreasing the markets for traditional media.

Recently, television has lost part of its audience share to growing reliance on the Internet for news and entertainment. Specifically, television's coveted prime-time programming now ranks second to Internet usage in audience share. In large part, audiences use the Internet for a variety of activities, including personal communication, information, and entertainment. But the growing market of video gaming and virtual gaming communities offer a form of entertainment that is more interactive and participatory then the passive viewing of a television program. One area of video gaming credited with securing greater audiences, particularly older audiences, is the popularity of online poker. Coincidentally, this phenomenon has also increased the popularity of television programs devoted to poker. As game developers continue to create interactive programs that tap into the personal interest of audiences, the gaming market will continue to grow. Further convergence between video games, the Internet, movies, and television, occupational opportunities in this area of New Media will mean more growth.

Production Designations and Descriptions

A list of occupations in New Media is detailed below. This list includes general descriptions of production positions in multimedia and New-Media production. Many of these occupations are specifically created by innovations in technology or changes in markets. (By definition, the term multimedia or New Media refers to the convergence of two or more forms of media, usually with a computer, and disseminated by the Internet, traditional forms of electronic media, or point-of-purchase displays.) The occupations outlined next are specific to the production of content and the outcome of a specific media product.

ANIMATOR—Animators create two-dimensional (2D) and three-dimensional (3D) images for illustrative purposes. Originally created with pen and paper, these types of illustrations are now created with the use of computer software. Animators work in a variety of industries such as motion picture, television, video game, and advertising.

ART DIRECTOR—An art director is responsible for the overall artistic guidance or content of a particular project. The art director maintains the consistency, quality, and uniformity of the production or project. The requirements or specific responsibilities of the art director vary in each industry.

GRAPHIC DESIGNER—A graphic designer will work on various components of a project, such as designing the virtual characters, backgrounds, screen layouts, menus, icons, buttons, and any other art relevant to the project. A graphic designer chooses the fonts that are used and the layout of the elements. Although the graphic designer includes the talents of an artist, skills in computer usage and software skills are necessary. The graphic designer may create original artwork for a project or production.

PROGRAMMER—The programmer writes computer code that is the foundation for computer programs, applications, or web pages. The programmer works with a variety of computer languages, such as C++, Java, and HTML. In some cases, programmers work from existing electronic or programming tools; at other times they must design applications from the ground up. Occupations in programming require an advanced level of computer proficiency.

SOUND PRODUCER—The sound producer designs and creates the audio content for media applications and productions. This position is responsible for all aspects of sound in the production, including music, dialogue, and sound effects. Because rich and textured audio contributes considerable realism and atmosphere to media productions, the work of the sound producer is critical to a project.

VIDEO PRODUCER—The video producer develops and produces the video elements in multimedia projects. The video producer oversees the story development, shooting, and editing of the footage to be incorporated into the project. The video producer is also in charge of converting the video footage into a digital format that is applicable to multimedia. Personnel employed in traditional video production occupations can adapt their abilities and skills to the New-Media and multimedia environment.

WRITERS—The writers is responsible for the narrative development of the multimedia application or project. The writer oversees the development of dialogue, character situations, voice-overs, and any text relevant to the production. Like video producers, writers employed in traditional media occupations may also adapt their talents to occupations in New-Media and multimedia production.

Conclusion

As personal computers, portable media devices, wireless technologies, and the Internet continue to see increases in usage and new applications, new outlets for interactive media and productions will create growth in occupational opportunities for developers of multimedia and New Media. Additionally, traditional media production occupations will continue to decline as these industries continue to adapt and implement digital technologies and rely on computers for production and dissemination.

R·E·F·E·R·E·N·C·E·S

Day, Louis Alvin. *Ethics in Media Communication,* Fifth Edition, Wadsworth, 2006.

Dolan, Michael. "The Future of Video Gaming." The Video Game Revolution. 25 Oct. 2005 <www.pbs.org>.

Jenkins, Henry. "Reality Bytes: Eight Myths About Video Games Debunked." The Video Game Revolution. MIT. 25 Oct. 2005 <www.pbs.org>.

Kindem, Gorham, and Robert B. Musburger. *Introduction to Media Production.* Third Edition. Focal Press, 2005.

"Netflix to Deliver Direct to TV." Jan. 3, 2008. <Time.com>.

"New Music Chart for Ringtones." BBC News. 31 May 2005. 25 Oct. 2005 <http://news.bbc.co.uk>.

Occupational Outlook Handbook, 2008–2009. U.S. Department of Labor, Bureau of Labor Statistics. <www.bls.gov/oco/cg/cgs017.htm>.

Peters, Oliver. "Developing a Desktop DI." *Videography.* Sept. 2005: 22–25.

"Podcasting." Wikipedia. 25 Oct. 2005 <http://wikipedia.com>.

"Professional Occupations in Multimedia." *California Occupational Guide.* 25 Oct. 2005. <www.calmis.ca.gov>.

"RSS (file format)." Wikipedia. 25 Oct. 2005. <http://wikipedia.com>.

CHAPTER

8 Advertising and Public Relations

Introduction

Occupations in advertising and public relations are often categorized as one industry, but their qualifications and occupational designations differ. Advertising companies work with clients to develop and implement advertising campaigns and strategies to market and promote products and services. Public relations firms coordinate and organize campaigns to promote an interest or image for their clients. Although the mission of both industries is to influence an audience or group, occupational designations differ slightly. According to the U.S. Bureau of Labor Statistics (2008), the advertising and public relations services industry employed 458,000 workers, and an additional 48,000 were self-employed in 2008.

Advertising

Advertising agencies offer a wide range of services to their clients, including creating and producing an advertising campaign for a variety of media outlets. At times, the audiences for some campaigns can be extremely segmented. The ad agencies write copy, prepare artwork and graphics, and provide any other creative work required for disseminating campaigns to radio, television, print, billboards, direct-to-mail, or the Internet. Some advertising agencies work with specific areas of media, while other agencies offer a broader variety of services and outlets for their clients.

The skills required to work in advertising are as varied as the occupations within the industry. A highly competitive industry, advertising emphasizes skills in marketing, communication, art, and design, offer advantages to candidates seeking occupations in advertising. Many of these occupations require a bachelor's degree in the areas previously specified. Although a degree in business, communications, English, art, or journalism will increase the possibility of employment in advertising, it is not a guarantee. An advantage to college students in any advertising-related program is the opportunity to work as an intern, or in a cooperative program, with an established agency or firm.

A geographical consideration for working within this industry is the concentration of companies within larger metropolitan centers, specifically New York and Los Angeles. According to the Bureau of Labor Statistics (2008), "California and New York together account for about 1 in 5 firms and more than 1 in 4 workers in the industry." In addition to this statistic, 68 percent of all advertising agencies employ five or fewer employees, with great attrition or layoffs when accounts are lost or consolidated. As advertising agencies are hired to promote and increase sales of products and services, their clients expect results and exposure. If a campaign is not successful in achieving this objective, it is common for the agency to lose business, resulting in the loss of staff. Conversely, if an agency is successful with one campaign, it can translate into more business and prestige within the industry. Competition is keen, and competitors are mindful of trends and developments in the industry.

New Media and digital technologies have greatly affected occupations in media, and the Internet is one of the fastest-growing forms of advertising. As the trend of media consolidation and convergence continues to transform media, the advertising industry will also use more digital technology. As with many new forms of media, at its inception the Internet was not seen as a viable source of advertising revenue, or as effective for reaching large or mass audiences. Nevertheless, as more people come to rely on the Internet for information and entertainment, advertisers will find new consumer markets and audiences on the Internet and the sites people frequent. In fact, web ratings are now conducted to establish rates based on audience size and reach, similar to television, radio, and print. As media audiences continue to migrate to the Internet as a primary source of information and entertainment, advertisers must adapt too. Skills in digital technologies and multimedia will therefore be in greater demand for occupations in the advertising industry.

Public Relations

Public relations (PR) firms differ slightly from their advertising agency counterparts. Although they are related in their objective to persuade and influence an audience or group, a public relations firm's goals are not achieved by the sale of a product or service. PR firms attempt to influence an audience or group's opinion, attitude, or interest concerning a business, political issue, or institution. PR personnel function as advisors throughout this process. The methods used are similar to those of advertising. Various forms of media are used to convey a point of view, or to adjust a public image. Most often, PR firms utilize written or printed forms of media, but electronic media is being used to a greater extent. Computer technologies and the Internet are particularly useful in public relations applications.

Public relations firms work as an intermediary between a client and their audience or group. As in advertising, success in influencing a group's opinion or attitude must be skillfully and cleverly crafted. A successful PR campaign may employ one or several approaches to achieve a positive outcome. Some successful strategies might include writing press releases, taking out advertisements in print media, arranging interviews with radio and television, sponsoring events, distributing direct mail, or more recently, utilizing the Internet and email. Email is becoming increasingly effective and cost efficient in getting a message or opinion out to a targeted audience. Because no one strategy is suited for every application, creativity and experience are relevant in designing and implementing an effective PR campaign. For this reason, the PR industry values experience as much as education. Compared to the advertising industry, PR firms have fewer employees and rely on successful campaigns to sustain a companies' list of clients. Reputations in both advertising and public relations are highly regarded and scrutinized.

Personal Profile: *Lacy Adams Dixon*

Name, job title, place of employment, and city/state?

Lacy Dixon, Director of Tourism & Convention Sales, Valdosta–Lowndes County Convention & Visitors Bureau, Valdosta, Georgia

Job duties?

I promote Valdosta-Lowndes County as a tourism destination through conferences, conventions, sporting events, family reunions, weddings, etc.

What is a typical day like?

My typical day varies dependent upon what we are currently working on. I might be planning a conference for a group coming in 2012 or hosting 9 meeting planners here in Valdosta to showcase our community, or helping the sports commission put on a triathlon.

How did you obtain your job?

I saw an advertisement for [the] job in the VDT in April 2004 and the rest is history!

Job search tips, hints, advice, or anecdotes?

I would say start with whom you know—friends or family—do they know of any available jobs, have any contacts, etc.

The skills necessary for occupations in public relations are comparable to those valued by the advertising industry. A bachelor's degree is requisite for most positions in a PR firm. Other qualities that enhance a person's qualifications are effective written and verbal skills, creativity, analytical skills or the ability to solve problems, and the ability to manage and work with others. As with advertising, college programs in public relations offer an advantage to an individual seeking employment in PR. These programs typically offer internship and cooperative opportunities with established PR firms, and in some cases, corporations. Additionally, associations such as the Public Relations Society of America (PRSA) accredit many college programs. Although there are not many full-fledged public relations college programs, students in such programs have a distinct advantage over students in other disciplines that have aspirations to work in the public relations industry.

Job Outlook

According to the Bureau of Labor Statistics (2008), occupations in advertising and public relations are predicted to grow by 13.6 percent over the next ten years. This is slightly higher than the 10.4 percent increase predicted for all industries over the same period. As the number of media outlets increases, so will occupations and opportunities in these related industries. With new media outlets, specifically the Internet, RSS, podcasting, weblogs, and the increasing use of portable media devices, there will be a need to advertise and influence consumers in order to subsidize the growing cost of materials and content.

Advertising was an innovative solution to the problem of finding funding for programming. From its use in print journalism, radio, television, and now the Internet, advertising has generated considerable revenue for media producers and the companies marketing their products or services. Changes in technology have signaled a change to this formula. With the proliferation of personal media devices, mass marketing is not practical or relevant to newer methods of media delivery. The development of innovative methods of dissemination may decrease the higher-than-average expectation in occupational growth.

The advertising industry has begun using new techniques and finding creative solutions to the decline of mass media markets. For example, Internet advertising now targets specific messages via cellular phones and RSS syndication feeds for consumers. Audiences who use these forms of media may or may not find the advertising messages relevant or useful, but the industry has embraced the need to take advantage of new technologies to deliver its message. In addition to new media, advertising agencies are finding ways to place products within many other forms of media, such as television shows, video games, and motion pictures. This form of advertising, known as product placement, is becoming prevalent and is known to be effective. As the advertising industry continues to develop new and innovative approaches to marketing products and services, job growth should increase as predicted.

Occupational Designations and Descriptions

A list of occupations in advertising and public relations is detailed below. The positions are general descriptions of jobs available within both areas.

ACCOUNT MANAGER—An account manager is responsible for finding clients for an agency or firm. It is also the account manager's responsibility to represent the agency to the client and oversee the campaign and quality of the work. The account manager's ultimate responsibility is to ensure the success of a campaign. This position may be found utilized in both advertising and public relations.

CREATIVE DIRECTOR—The creative director oversees the creative services provided by an agency or firm. This includes copy writing, artwork, graphics, and any work related to the creative development within a campaign. The creative director also manages the respective staff involved in the creative execution of a campaign. Creative directors are found in both advertising and public relations.

MEDIA DIRECTOR—The media director oversees the communications media and staff for a particular campaign. The media director plans and chooses the personnel who will produce a campaign for radio, television, print media, and the Internet. The media director position may be found in both advertising and public relations.

PUBLIC RELATIONS MANAGER—The public relations manager oversees campaigns for various clients in a PR firm. PR managers usually specialize in a particular area or industry.

PUBLIC RELATIONS SPECIALIST—A public relations specialist is responsible for specific functions within a PR campaign, such as media, community, consumer, and government relations. A PR specialist works on political campaigns, corporate relations, interest group relations, and other issues concerning a client's interest.

COPYWRITERS—A copywriter writes the actual ads or copy for an advertising campaign, including scripts for radio and television campaigns.

ART DIRECTOR—An art director is responsible for executing the visual concepts and designs of an advertising campaign. The art director is also responsible for storyboards or production design for television campaigns.

GRAPHIC DESIGNERS—Graphic designers execute the print, electronic, and film media utilized in an advertising campaign.

RESEARCH EXECUTIVES—Research executives compile the data used to develop a strategy or marketing plan for a campaign. Their primary responsibility is collecting information that will ensure the success of a campaign. Other responsibilities include monitoring the effectiveness of a particular campaign. This information can vary from predicting past and future sales of products to polling information concerning a political candidates chance's of winning an election. Research executives are utilized in both advertising and public relations.

Conclusion

Although occupations in advertising and Public Relations are not directly responsible for media production, this industry serves as an intermediary to the production process. Occupations in advertising and public relations are integral to the content development of most areas of media production. Advertising is the economic engine that drives most popular media. Without this symbiotic relationship, popular entertainment and informational programming could not subsist. Conversely, individuals seeking occupations in advertising and public relations are expected to work within the media production environment and must understand the roles and responsibilities of personnel in the production setting.

Additionally, as technology continues to consolidate many areas of media production and dissemination, personnel in advertising and public relations will need to adapt to new production methods and distribution of media. In addition to the changes in production techniques, new media will affect audience's attitudes and values concerning advertising and PR campaign strategies. As commercial television and radio adapt to the use of Tivo and satellite radio, advertising personnel must reassess the traditional approaches to reaching and convincing audiences to buy a product or service.

R-E-F-E-R-E-N-C-E-S

"Advertising and Public Relations Services." U.S. *Bureau of Labor Statistics*. U.S. Department of Labor. 2006. <www.bls.gov>.

"Advertising, Marketing, Promotions, Public Relations and Sales Managers." *Career Information*. 1 Nov. 2005 <www.collegegrad.com>.

"Careers in Public Relations: An Overview." *The Public Relations Profession*. Public Relations Society of America. 1 Nov. 2005 <www.prsa.org>.

"Marketing, Advertising, and Public Relations Managers." University of Missouri, St. Louis. 1 Nov. 2005 <www.umsl.edu>.

"Public Relations Representatives." *California Occupational Guide*. State of California, Employment Development Department. 1 Nov. 2005 <www.calmis.ca.gov>.

CHAPTER

9 Educational Media

Interconnecting Mass Media and Education

To a large extent, media and education are intertwined. Employers want to hire educated candidates, preferably those who have college degrees. And the educational fields are relying more heavily on the media profession to help instruct students. The purpose of this chapter is twofold: (1) to examine the educational choices that prepare one for a career in media and (2) to document how a media background can lend itself to employment in education.

Media outreach programs via distance education, telecommunication courses, and educational access channels on cable television present other viable models of employment. Potential employees often overlook these fields. Yet they remain feasible alternatives to the standard positions in traditional broadcasting or corporate production models.

Educational Choices

Undergraduate Programs

According to the Bureau of Labor Statistics (2008), more than 1,500 institutions offer programs in communications, journalism, and related subjects. In 2007, 109 of these were accredited by the Accrediting Council on Education in Journalism and Mass Communications. A college campus may have thousands of students, most of whom are working toward an undergraduate degree. These degrees are most commonly the B.A. (Bachelor of Arts) or B.S. (Bachelor of Science). Other programs relevant to the communications field are the B.F.A. (Bachelor of Fine Arts) and the B.J. (Bachelor of Journalism). Some degrees, notably the B.B.A. (Bachelor of Business Administration), are particularly well suited for those seeking careers in the sales and management of media.

Appendix A lists many of the undergraduate programs relevant in mass communication and journalism across the country. Potential applicants should note that the degrees can be dissimilar, as colleges may focus their curricula on telecommunications, broadcast journalism, video production, or another related field. This is of particular concern when students may be more suited to earn a B.F.A. in Radio-TV-Film but instead find themselves in a B.S. in Communications.

Graduate Programs

The number of universities offering graduate degrees related to communications varies by specialization. Gradschool.com, for example, lists 99 graduate programs in Media Studies, 129 in Radio-Television-Film, and 330 in Journalism and Mass Media. Given the broad range of programs in communications, prospective students should carefully seek out those schools that mirror their professional interests.

Far too often, undergraduate students with no career plan opt for an advanced degree. However, graduate school should never be looked upon as a mere fallback plan, as the time and effort to obtain an advanced degree is substantial. A typical Master's program requires a minimum of two years of study, and earning a Ph.D. can easily consume another five years. The end result of the advanced degree is an opportunity to teach and research in a mass communications program. It is worth noting, however, that the advanced degree does not necessarily impress those in the broadcast and production fields, which typically value work experience over education. Except for top-level film schools, such as USC, NYU, or the University of Texas, the graduate degree may not have equal weight in either production or academic fields.

The application process for graduate programs is rigorous, and requires transcripts, letters of recommendation, an application form, high marks on the Graduate Record Examinations (GRE), and a writing sample. Schools may also require supplemental material, such as samples of video productions or a letter of intent. Graduate schools have early deadlines, usually in the winter preceding a fall admission. Most programs start only in the fall, unlike undergraduate programs, which accept students during any term.

Statistically, the ratio of applicants to accepted students can rival that of medical or law schools. It is not uncommon for top programs to receive 400 applications for a dozen openings. Once in graduate school, a student usually completes the coursework in two to three years. This is followed by the thesis or dissertation, a graduate-level project that may take up to five years to complete. As noted earlier, potential students who look to graduate school as a safety net for employment in the real world should evaluate their career path with intense scrutiny.

Terminal and Non-Terminal Degrees

The distinction between terminal and non-terminal degrees is imperative for those interested in graduate programs. The terminal degree is usually the doctorate in the field, but there are a few exceptions. In mass communications, the Master of Fine Arts degree is regarded as terminal in the areas of production or creative writing. The doctorates in the field are the Ph.D. and the Ed.D. (Doctor of Education). The Ph.D. lends itself to research and criticism of the discipline, while the Ed.D. can be used to merge education and mass communication. A Master of Arts, the most common graduate degree offered, is a nonterminal degree. However, one must have a Master of Arts in hand before pursuing a doctoral program. Those interested in the M.F.A. do not need the M.A. first and may enter following completion of an undergraduate program.

Employment in Academia

Positions at Colleges and Universities

With a graduate degree in hand, students find the world of academic employment open to them. There are thousands of community colleges, state universities, and private schools that are potential employers, although not all offer specialized programs in mass communications, broadcast journalism, video production, or a related field. Even schools without these degree programs, however, tend to offer courses in basic communication or mass communication. In 2006, there were 29,000 instructors, lecturers, and professors teaching at postsecondary colleges (Bureau of Labor Statistics, 2008).

Personal Profile: *Shana Dean Young*

Name, title, place of employment, and city/state?

Shana Dean Young, M.A., Assistant Director, The Leadership Institute, Cunningham Center for Leadership Development, Columbus State University, Columbus, Georgia

Job duties

Assisting in strategic planning for the Leadership Institute to include program development, goal setting, and progress tracking to measure impact of efforts. Coordination, communication, and promotion of the Leadership Institute as well as assisting in the development and implementation of professional development programs in a variety of formats. In addition to the corporate leadership and professional development training, I also assist in the coordination of several major conferences put on by the Cunningham Center for Leadership Development (i.e., The Jim Blanchard Leadership Forum, The Women's Leadership Development Conference, The Young Professionals Conference, and The Poverty Symposium).

What is a typical day like?

Every day is different: I could be facilitating a course on Communication and Leadership at Work for a Client, doing a one-on-one consultation or coaching session for an individual; Researching and reading to develop a new leadership course; administering one of the many leadership assessments we offer; Depending on the time of year I could be . . . coordinating an upcoming conference (hiring speakers, breakout session leaders, deciding on the conference format, assisting in creating materials for distribution concerning the conference at hand, recruiting attendees, meeting with possible sponsors, and organizing everything from how the speaker is going to get here and where they are going to stay, down to what kind of food we are going to serve and how the name tags are going to look).

How did you obtain your job?

Prior to being hired for my current position I was an Assistant Professor in the Communication Department here at Columbus State University. The Cunningham Center recruited me to be the first Assistant Director of the Leadership Institute in August of 2007.

Personal Profile: *Shana Dean Young (continued)*

Job search tips, hints, advice, or anecdotes?

Be honest in your representation of yourself and your abilities (don't oversell and then under deliver). Know and be able to clearly identify your weaknesses and how you are working on them. Love what you do—if you don't, you will make yourself and everyone else around you miserable (including your co-workers and your family). Be flexible, accept the fact that change is inevitable in any line of work and embrace it. Choosing a first job where there is a lot of travel involved is great! I did and in 2 years had been everywhere in the United States. I had always wanted to travel to Los Angeles, New York, San Francisco, San Diego, Chicago, and so on. You get to go, see, and do before you start a family. These jobs are usually easier for recent college graduates to obtain simply because most people with spouses and children don't want to be on the road a lot. Seriously, be careful what you or anyone else puts on the Internet about yourself (i.e., My Space, Facebook, and the like). Nothing is ever truly "gone" from the Internet and if savvy IT personnel are instructed to look for it, they will find it. Get involved in the community in which you plan to live. Join a Young Professionals program in the area to get to know people if you move to an unfamiliar place.

Salary

$50,000 to $60,000

Personal Profile: *Christi Chase*

Name, job title, place of employment, and city/state?

My name is Christi Chase and I am currently employed in Kuwait at the American School of Kuwait.

What are your job duties?

I am an English language teacher and provide screenwriting and production writing seminars for the middle and high school writing conferences. My job as a language teacher is to provide students who do not speak the English language with support and language skills they can use in the classroom. During my seminars, my duty is to provide the students a chance to understand the techniques and thought process behind the screen-writing format and to help them develop their ideas into a working screenplay.

What is a typical day like?

A typical day during my seminar involves a morning session of brainstorming ideas and developing a working plot. The afternoon session involves working with screenwriting software to begin writing in the screenwriting format. We continue with character development, treatment writing, and outlining to help the writing process.

Personal Profile: *Christi Chase (continued)*

How did you obtain your job?

I found the job online doing a search for teaching positions in Kuwait and adapted what I learned from screenwriting into a working presentation that I present to my students and to other teachers through conferences in the area. After working for a radio station, I realized that I most enjoyed teaching and working with kids.

Job search tips, hints, advice, or anecdotes?

I advise any seeking a position in any field in media to use networking and communication skills, do an internship, and don't worry about where the money is coming from. In other words, take advantage of an offer and worry about the details later.

Salary

The salary range depends on the currency exchange rate on any given day. Because I work outside of the United States, I am not subjected to taxes on my income. My housing and utilities are paid for in my contract, as well as all of my health insurance and benefits. The range of my cash salary is somewhere between $36,000 and $40,000.

Introductory positions in academics consist of lecturers, instructors, and assistant professors. Instructors and lecturers are often temporary and don't possess the same research and production responsibilities as assistant professors. Those with Master of Arts degrees can receive a position as an instructor, but an assistant professor job is usually out of reach, unless the applicant has a wealth of experience.

Assistant professor positions are generally reserved for those with a terminal degree. Universities offer these to groom faculty for long-term employment, with the next steps of employment being associate professor and full professor. The requirements for advancement vary by institution, but as a broad guideline, the school will require excellence in teaching, service, research, or creative production.

Tenure is another benefit to employment in academics. Assistant professors' positions are frequently advertised as being tenure-track. This means the applicant is given five to seven years to prove himself or herself worthy of tenure. If the applicant excels in the position, the university may award tenure, which is a commitment to continued employment that can only be revoked for justifiable cause.

For a nine-month teaching position, the "2007–2008 National Salary Survey Results" published by the Broadcast Education Association reported the following average salaries for those teaching electronic media production:

Rank	Low Salary	High Salary	Median Salary
Instructor	$28,924	$68,859	$43,000
Assistant Professor	37,988	79,000	52,727
Associate Professor	43,154	124,600	62,093
Full Professor	48,000	192,374	82,394

Source: Broadcast Education Association, 2007.

Personal Profile: *Samantha Harden*

Name, job title, place of employment, and city/state?

Sam Harden, teacher, Colquitt County High School, Moultrie, Georgia

Job duties?

I teach students the various aspects of video and audio production. Oftentimes, I am asked to do "special projects."

What is a typical day like?

I begin teaching at 8:05 a.m. I have 6 classes. Four of these classes are intro classes. The students enjoy getting their feet wet, so to speak. Every day, they come into the room and ask if they get to go outside (this means use the field cameras). I have an advanced class that puts out a weekly show, "CHANNEL PACK." They have to write scripts, edit, and produce the show with guidance from me. We are also introducing radio this year. It is not up and running, but hopefully by Christmas 2008 we will have a station. Needless to say, I have a busy schedule and sometimes it is very difficult because kids will always be kids, and of course know more than you.

How did you obtain your job?

I was already teaching middle school reading. Then this job came open, and I was like, "Hey, I might be able to do that. I mean I did go to school for it and everything." I went for an interview, and I like to say my charm won them over, but I think it was my experience and possible contacts at Valdosta State that really landed the gig for me.

Job search tips, hints, advice, or anecdotes?

I wish I did have some words of wisdom. I had been out of the business for 11 years before I got this job. A lot has changed in that time. If I did have one bit of advice, it would be to hang in there. Someone is always looking for help with something in the video world. Keep your ears open and your feet wet, and eventually something will come your way because people will have heard about you.

Salary

Around $60,000.

According to the same survey, the average for an incoming instructor without prior full-time teaching experience was $39,779, and the average salary for an incoming assistant professor who had just completed the terminal degree was $51,336.

Positions at Middle and High Schools

Positions teaching media, broadcast journalism, and related fields are available at many middle and high schools nationwide, but applicants should be cognizant of budgetary concerns. Media programs are often among the first to be curtailed at these institutions since their educational outcomes may not specifically correspond with state-mandated requirements.

Most teachers in these programs specialize in media or broadcast journalism, but also instruct in related fields, such as English. Supervising the school newspaper or yearbook is a common job requirement.

In 2006, the median annual salary of kindergarten, elementary, middle, and secondary schoolteachers ranged between $43,580 and $48,690 (Bureau of Labor Statistics, 2008). This average reflects all teachers' salaries regardless of seniority or experience. According to the American Federation of Teachers (2008), beginning teachers with a bachelor's degree earned an average of $31,753 in the 2004–2005 school year.

School libraries also use media for instructional purposes, which led to the development of library technician and media aide positions. These jobs do not focus on media, but rather use the field as a supplement to the library's educational mission. Many media aides and library technicians spend much of their time performing typical library tasks, such as shelving books and monitoring circulation. In elementary and secondary schools in 2006, the average salary for library technicians was $24,760, while library technicians at colleges averaged $29,950. That position with the federal government in 2007 averaged $43,238 (Bureau of Labor Statistics, 2008).

Distance Learning and Access Channels

The production of distance learning courses varies greatly: some are simply a teacher standing in front of a digital camera; the data is then streamed to students at their home computers via the Internet. Other distance learning facilities have full studios and require camera operators, directors, stage managers, and other related positions. Jobs in these facilities mirror the studio setting found in corporate production. Given the potential cost savings of cable casting a lecture to a home audience, distance education has made great inroads as a viable alternative to traditional classroom education.

Access channels are another venue for employment. These channels are known as Public, Educational, and Government (PEG) channels. PEG channels are not mandated by federal law. Instead, their existence is negotiated between the cable company and the franchising authority, which is the city or country government. According to the Alliance for Community Media (2008), thousands of community groups and over one million volunteer producers, directors, presenters, and technical staff participate in PEG-access production annually. These volunteers produce more than 20,000 hours of new local programming each week. That is more than all the programming produced by NBC, CBS, ABC, FOX, and PBS combined. Among the three types of access channels, the public channels vary the greatest amount, with some cable systems providing free field and studio equipment to the public. At the other end of the spectrum, some cable systems may have a channel open for airing productions, but provide no video gear.

Local universities or school systems usually run educational channels, while government the franchising authority maintains channels. Because there are different levels of funding and support at these channels, job possibilities exist at various levels.

Personal Profile: *Jade Bulecza*

Name, title, place of employment, and city/state?

Jade Bulecza, Media Coordinator, City of Valdosta, Valdosta, Georgia

Job duties?

I produce all programming and bulletin information for Metro Valdosta Channel 96, a government access channel for the City of Valdosta. Here, I host In Focus Valdosta, a 30-minute program highlighting the City of Valdosta's events and services. I'm nearly a one-man show.

What is a typical day like?

My day varies: I could be shooting interviews, writing scripts, supervising interns, editing, or hosting a show. It's never boring.

How did you obtain your job?

I interned here. An internship gives you great real-world experience, and in some cases you can land a job, like I did.

Job search tips, hints, advice, or anecdotes?

When job searching, apply months in advance and don't get discouraged. I've heard the average person goes on 15 interviews before getting hired.

Salary

My salary ranges between $20,000 and $30,000.

Conclusion

Given the connections between education and the mass media, employment opportunities exist both for those who are furthering their academic study in the field, as well as those who are teaching via access channels and distance education. Due to the different levels of support for media practitioners within secondary education and community PEG channels, jobs should be researched on a local level to ascertain the employment environment of a specific community.

There is ample opportunity for those seeking employment in post-secondary education. There are hundreds of degree programs in the field, as well as those offering only basic instruction as part of a larger undergraduate core curriculum, provide ample opportunity for academic careers. As a prerequisite for those positions, successful graduates should thoroughly examine graduate programs and the wide variety of specializations they offer.

REFERENCES

"Alliance for Community Media." *Quick Facts on Media Access.* 18 July 2008 <www.ourchannels.org/?page_id=4>.

Gradschools.com. 18 July 2008 <http://www.bls.gov/oco/ocos069.htm>.

Orlik, Peter B. "2007–2008 National Salary Survey Results." *Broadcast Education Association.* Fall, 2007. Central Michigan University. 18 June 2008 <www.beaweb.org/04news/salsur.html>.

U.S. Bureau of Labor Statistics. 18 July 2008 <www.bls.gov/oco/ocos066.htm>, <www.bls.gov/oco/ocos069.htm>, < www.bls.gov/oco/ocos088.htm>, <www.bls.gov/oco/ocos113.htm>.

10 Portfolio Development

Competition in the Job Market

More than 1,500 institutions in the United States offer undergraduate degrees, including four-year programs at large universities, two-year curricula at two-year community colleges, and trade schools that offer training in course packages lasting as little as six months (Digest of Education Statistics, 2007). Given these numbers, it is imperative that those seeking employment present their application materials in as professional a manner as possible.

With the ease of creating websites, a number of job seekers now publish pages of their own work, allowing prospective employers to evaluate the work samples at any time. Still, the employer needs to be able to access the website, meaning prior contact must be made to provide the employer with the website's digital address.

The limits of traditional job searches meant mailing samples of work to prospective employers, but technology is shifting that paradigm as well. Some employers now request that cover letters and written materials to be sent via email, while samples of audio and work may be attached to an email as digital files. The job listing should specify which submission technique the company prefers. The following discussion will concentrate on portfolios that are physically delivered to the prospective employer.

Portfolios

Portfolios for the media professions consist of three separate items: (1) samples of your previous work, (2) a resume, and (3) a cover letter. Two of the items in a portfolio, the resume and cover letter, are universal among job applicants, while the examples of previous work varies depending on the industry. Finally, writing samples may also be required; while these are not mandatory for a portfolio, they may be encountered during the job interview process. This section will provide a discussion of each, as well as samples and reference points.

Samples of previous work are the most important part of a job search. A media-hiring manager will forgive a less-than-perfect grade point average and not participating in student groups. Nevertheless, excellent samples of previous work supersede all else and can get an applicant in the door and poor ones will keep one out.

Samples of Previous Work

Audio Demo Tapes

The audio CD presents the highlights of your audio career and lasts for less than ten minutes. While still referred to as a demo tape, audio applicants now take advantage of CD or DVD recording technology for their portfolios. You may have several air checks in a row at the beginning of the CD, with short pauses lasting no more than two seconds between them.

Start with an audio montage. It should last between 45 seconds and one minute and contain short audio clips of your on-air work. This montage gives the listener a chance to hear a quick overview of your delivery. Following the audio montage, several more extended air checks are presented. The type of air check varies according to the format played by the potential employer's format. For news personalities, the audio CD typically contains several recent newscasts. For disc jockeys, there are a variety of elements that can be used, including extended air checks, production work, interviews with musicians, or live remotes. In all cases, the voice heard on the demo work must be engaging, friendly, and in the case of news personalities, authoritative.

The entire audio demo tape (or CD) should last between eight and ten minutes. Once completed, it is vital that the CD is reviewed, as skips and scratches can ruin an audio CD and a first impression. Once the CD is approved, it should be professionally labeled and delivered in a professional container.

Tearsheets and Campaigns

A tearsheet or clipping is a sample of published writing that has been cut from the newspaper or magazine in which it appeared, such as a college newspaper. For applicants in the print media, tearsheets, or clippings, demonstrate competence in writing skills. The clippings should be mounted into a three ring binder and presented in plastic sleeves to prevent damage from handling. If the samples do not include the title and date of the original publication, those references should be added.

Applicants in public relations must illustrate their ability to work in the field, as demonstrated through their history with public relations campaigns. PR practitioners typically prepare written materials, such as brochures, articles, press releases, and newsletters. Other items, such as videotapes, PowerPoint presentations, and audio samples, can be used in a portfolio. All samples should be professionally displayed, regardless of their format.

Video Demo Reels

Unless a job posting specifies what format is preferred for the demo reel, it is preferred to send a DVD. Although most news directors typically have access to VHS players, DVD demo reels are quickly replacing videotapes as the format of choice. Professional formats, like DVC-Pro or Beta SP, should be avoided for resume tapes; they are too expensive to send out, plus the news director likely will not have access to that playback format outside of the station's master control office.

It is not uncommon for a news director to receive more than 100 demo reels for a single on-air position. In addition, news directors may have stacks of applications that were sent in without jobs being posted. No news director can physically watch all submitted video samples from start to finish—there are simply too many submissions to manage. Most news directors will watch the demo reel for at least 30 seconds, and if the candidate is unsuitable, they move on. Some news directors are known to stop demos as soon as they have seen the first frame of the montage—If the person does not have "the look," they want there is no point in watching more.

The video reel is the most vital piece of the portfolio. Like the audio reel, it lasts only eight to ten minutes. During this brief time, you need to consolidate the best work from college classes, independent productions, freelance gigs, and previous jobs. Since every second of viewing time counts, the reel should follow certain guidelines to ensure the news director will watch the entire product and then contact the job applicant. The demo reel starts with a video slate.

A typical order of what appears on a demo is as follows:

Order on Tape	Item on Tape	Duration, in seconds
1	Introductory Slate	:10 to :15
2	On-Air Montage	:30 to :40
3	First News Story	1:00 to 1:30
4	Second News Story	1:00 to 1:30
5	Third News Story	1:00 to 1:30
6	Fourth News Story	1:00 to 1:30
7	Fifth News Story	1:00 to 1:30
8	End Slate	:10 to :15
Total Running Time		5:50 to 8:40 minutes

No more than a second or two of black should be placed between the slate, montage, and each story. The segments should have enough black to give the viewer a visual break between the stories, but not enough time to prompt the viewer to stop the reel.

Introductory Slate

The first image a news director should see on the video reel is the introductory slate, which includes the candidate's contact information. The slate lasts between 10 and 15 seconds and consists of either a computer-generated background or a frozen video image of the applicant with contact information graphically superimposed on top of that image. The same rules apply to the slate as for a cover letter—make sure the information is accurate, professional, and easy to read. The slate should include the following information:

- Name
- Phone Numbers
- Street Address
- Email Address

Phone numbers and street addresses may be problematic, as graduating students may move from an on-campus address. The simple rule of thumb is that applicants should use the contact information where they can be reached. Plan so that the address will be available for receipt of future deliveries. If a student is moving out of the dormitory upon graduation, they should list the address where they will eventually reside.

It is customary for the student to retain their university or college email address for a period of six months to a full year after graduation. Applicants should use either the university email address or a generic one at a service like yahoo, hotmail, or gmail. Avoid using a social email address that does not look professional. Plan to check email messages at least every other day.

The job candidate should put the slate at the beginning of the reel to show the news director what they look like. The identical slate should be placed at the end of the reel to give closure to the submission, as well as to remind the viewer how to make contact.

Video Samples for the Demo Reel

Preparing the demo reel means condensing one's broadcast history into an average of six to eight minutes (less than ten minutes). The job seeker must review all of his or her video samples in order to select the best ones. Ideally, the applicant should "rough out" the resume tape on paper first, making an ever-shortening list of material. All material should be critically screened for writing flaws, production errors, and less-than-stellar work.

On-air personalities should gather two types of material: (1) stand-ups that can be used in an introductory montage and (2) their best news packages. Most news packages run a minute to 1:30 in duration, so four or five pieces will fit on the demo reel. Material should be ranked in order from best to worst. When evaluating stories, remember that raging fires or screaming car chases do not always impress news directors, since from an editorial viewpoint, those stories are relatively easy to cover. However, well-covered stories on school board meetings or zoning hearings are of greater interest to news directors. Since reporters will not have a catastrophe to cover every day, news directors need to see how applicants can develop stories from regular daily events.

Next, an applicant should evaluate remaining stand-ups or on-air tags for any that merit inclusion. These should be from stories that will not appear in whole on the demo. These will form an introductory montage, which will appear after the slate and before the four to five news stories. Most news directors want a quick montage of five to eight different stand-ups or on-air tags to see applicants in different situations, wearing different clothes, to get an idea of how the person will look on a daily basis.

Once all tapes are collected and prioritized, they can be copied to the demo.

DVD Samples

For a DVD, the process is slightly different. The main screen, which doubles as your introductory slate, should also list the stories. Since DVDs can present stories in different sequences, one can either rank the stories in a column on one side of the screen or simply place the stories on different areas. Ranking the stories in a column provides some marginal control over what story the news director clicks on first, but the difference between your "best" and "worst" stories on the DVD needs to be much smaller. The news director may prefer to watch the last video story on the list instead of following the order presented on-screen. Simply put, every story must be worthy.

Once edited, a professional label should be affixed to the DVD or tape. If VHS tape is used, color bars, tone, and a countdown should be left out, as any of these may annoy the viewer. Instead, the tape should be cued to the start of introductory slate.

The Resume

Job placement services and career centers have bookshelves filled with sample resumes and cover letters, none of which agree on precise formats, style, or structure. Most word-processing programs have sample templates embedded in them, allowing the user to fill in the blanks to create a resume. Resume templates can pose problems, as some employers recognize the templates and that the applicant is simply too lazy to design an original resume.

There are basic guidelines to follow that are universal in resume development. First, each resume includes standard sections, such as the heading, work experience, and so forth. Second, the resume must be proofread for accuracy and grammar. Finally, the resume must be presented professionally on quality paper with traditional formats, such as 12-point Times New Roman font, black type, and printed on a white or cream colored, medium-stock page.

A number of employers now accept applications online, thus the resume will be copied and pasted electronically. This eliminates printing and mailing errors. However, each resume should still be checked for accuracy and clarity before submission.

Sections of a Resume

The typical resume includes standard sections, which are described next.

A. Heading
   1. Include name, address, phone number, and email address. Make sure the information is accurate and consistent with the contact information on the cover letter and the introductory slate.
   2. Alert anyone who may answer your phone (roommates, parents, friends) that you are expecting calls from potential employers. The person answering the phone should be professional and polite, and the person should be able to take accurate and complete messages.
   3. Be professional when answering your phone or recording the outgoing message—do not include background or use slang or sarcastic language.
B. Objective
   1. Be clear and concise. Simply state the position/career field for which you are applying.
   2. The objective is optional on the resume, but it must be stated on the cover letter.
C. Education
   1. Include your degree, major (minor) or program, school, and graduation date (month/year).
   2. Spell out the degree you are receiving. Include your GPA if it is 3.0 or higher. If your GPA is below 3.0, calculate the GPA you earned in your major classes and list it if it exceeds 3.0.
   3. You may also include a brief list of relevant upper-division courses that would help you in your position, such as Broadcast News Writing, Directing, Advanced Editing, Audio Design, and so on.

D. Work Experience
1. List your jobs in chronological order, beginning with the most recent.
2. Include the company's name, as well as the city and state in which it is located. List your title, dates of employment, and your job duties.
3. The job duties may be listed in paragraph form or in a bulleted list.

E. Skills
1. Skills are developed from paid employment, volunteer work, internships, activities, and coursework.
2. List any skills you have in customer service, software knowledge, leadership, foreign language, and so on.
3. Try to offer three to five skills that would be of interest to a potential employer.

F. Honors and Activities
1. Include any organizations or committees in which you have been involved.
2. Provide information on any offices that you have held or any other forms of leadership. These may be in bullet or paragraph form.
3. If you were not an officer but participated in an organization, note if you helped to organize any specific projects or conferences for the group.

G. References
1. Provide three to five professional references. Be sure to ask the individual if he or she can serve as a reference before listing them.
2. You may state "References available upon request" or leave that section off if it has not been requested in the job listing. However, be prepared to provide references during the interview.
3. If you include references with your resume, list them on a separate sheet of paper. Include the reference's name, title, organization, address, and phone number as shown.

> Mr./Mrs./Dr., First and Last Name, Title
> Organization
> Street Address
> City, State, Zip
> Telephone Number, including area code
> Email Address
> Relationship (Academic Advisor, Supervisor, etc.)

Reviewing the Resume

Once the information for the resume is written and formatted, use the following tips to ensure that your resume will appear professional.

DO	DON'T
Provide information that is positive and relevant to the job objective.	Provide the reader with your life history, or with negative information that is not required.
Make use of spacing, bolding, capitalization, italics, and indentation to make the resume visually appealing.	Overuse different fonts, graphics, etc., in a way that become distracting.
Try to limit yourself to one or two pages. The employer will not take the time to read your resume word for word and is not likely to glance at it if it is too lengthy.	Include information that is irrelevant simply to fill space. In addition, the resume is not a confessional. Do not include information that might be construed as negative if it is not required.
Use correct terminology related to the industry you are interested in.	Misuse words simply because it sounds impressive.
Proofread. Check your resume for grammar, punctuation, and spelling errors. Ask others to analyze it. If you have a Career Services office at your college, use their resume proofreading service if one is available to you.	Assume that the computer spell check will catch every mistake.
Leave out information regarding ethnicity, religion, marital status, and age.	Include a photograph or physical description of yourself.
Print resume on $8\frac{1}{2}'' \times 11''$ paper. White is preferred, but neutral colors are acceptable.	Use paper of an unusual size or color. Fluorescent colors, dark paper, and colored ink are not viewed as professional.

Sample Resumes

The next three pages include samples of professional resumes.

EDDIE MORGAN

8920 Main Street, Alpharetta, GA 30022

(404) 555-1212

eddiemorgan@valdosta.edu

Education

Valdosta State University, Valdosta, GA

Bachelor of Fine Arts, Mass Media. GPA 3.53 December, 2008

Professional Experience

Worked on production crews for ESPN, CBS Sports, and Jefferson Pilot Sports between 2005 and 2008

College Experience

Valdosta State University   **Valdosta, GA**

WVVS Valdosta 90.9 FM   *2006–2008*

- Host of two-hour weekly sports radio program highlighting VSU athletics, along with local, regional, and national news.
- Conducted live on-air interviews with players, coaches, and experts.
- Hosted weekly two-hour disc jockey shift.

VSU-TV, Channel 11   *2005–2008*

- Produced VSU football broadcasts
- Play-by-play announcer for VSU football, baseball, basketball teams.
- Host of 30-minute Blazer Sports Report television show highlighting all VSU athletic programs.
- Conducted television interviews with coaches and players.

The Spectator   *2006–2007*

- Sports writer/columnist for campus newspaper.
- Contributions includes previews, reviews, columns, and features

Honors and Activities

- 2008 National Society for Collegiate Journalists 1st place award—"VSU Football vs. SAU"
- 2007 National Society for Collegiate Journalists 1st place award—"VSU Football vs. UNA"
- National Dean's List; VSU Dean's List, eight consecutive semesters
- Captain, VSU Ultimate Frisbee 2006–2008

RAQUEL MOON
3258 East Brookwood Drive
Valdosta, GA 31602
(229) 555-1212
raquelmoon@valdosta.edu

OBJECTIVE   Seek a position as a production crew member

EDUCATION   *Bachelor of Fine Arts, Mass Media GPA 3.59*   *May 2009*
Valdosta State University   Valdosta GA

Internship

W.P. Productions   *Ray City, GA*   *Summer 2008*
- Edit PSAs for The Southern Company and episodes of "The Search for the Ultimate Outdoorsman," which aired on ESPN2
- Taped interviews with DVC Pro Camera, logged tapes, and conducted basic research

Collegiate Experience

Valdosta State University   **Valdosta, GA**

Satellite Services   *Summer 2007–present*
Student Assistant
- Produce, edit, and conduct remote shoots for University-related commercials and marketing tapes
- Camera operator for the Chris Hatcher Show, which is Valdosta's head football coach's after-the-game show.
- Director of classroom coverage that is recorded and mailed to graduate students

Blazer T.V.   *2006–present*
Director/Camera Operator/Instant Replay
- Set up cameras and video and audio cables prior to university athletic events
- Either direct, operate a camera, or run instant replay machine for sports coverage

VSU T.V.   *November 2006*
Director
- Directed Valdosta State's coverage of the 2006 elections. Received the honorable mention award at the 2007 Society for Collegiate Journalists National Convention.

ESPN   *Jacksonville, FL /Atlanta, GA*
Camera Assistant   *2007/2008 Football Seasons*
- Assist camera operators by running cables along the field during Jaguars and Falcons football games.

Ruth Marjorie Church

10639 Park Avenue   Valdosta, GA 31602

(229) 555-1212   ruthmchurch@valdosta.edu

Education

Bachelor of Fine Arts, Mass Media: Broadcast Journalism Emphasis

Valdosta State University, Valdosta, GA, May 2009

Professional Experience

WUPA UPN 69, Atlanta, GA

Internship, Summer 2008

- Assisted with live productions on production truck.
- Provided staff support at *America's Next Top Model* Casting Call, Vibe Music Festival, and Music Midtown.

Focus Atlanta, Atlanta, GA

Production Assistant, Summer 2007

- Booked guests, screened phone calls.
- Developed and researched feature stories reflecting community interests.
- Served as Director, Audio Supervisor, Videographer, and Floor Director.

RTG Media, Valdosta, GA

Radio Personality—Hot 102.7, 2006–Present

- Produce and perform mid-day show.
- Assist with live remotes.
- Produce commercials and Public Service Announcements.

VSU News 11, Valdosta, GA

Anchor/Reporter, 2005–Present

- Generated and researched story ideas.
- Worked as anchor and reporter for national award-winning news series.
- Videotaped and edited stories for live broadcasts.

Technical Expertise

Proficient with Canon Digital GL Series, DVC Pro, and Avid Non-linear Editing System

Activities

Vice President, VSU Student Chapter, National Broadcasting Society

Volunteers: Big Brothers Big Sisters and Hurricane Katrina Fundraiser

The Cover Letter

A cover letter is essential when you are not able to personally deliver your resume to a prospective employer. Your cover letter should be personal and convey to the reader what you know about the employer and how you will best fit in with the organization. The letter should be three to four paragraphs in length and should fulfill four goals:

1. *Introductory Paragraph.* The first paragraph should contain information on the position you are applying for and how you discovered the position (such as through a newspaper ad, mutual acquaintance, or webpage). If the position has not been advertised, then this paragraph should state the type of position you are interested in and summarize for the reader the characteristics of the organization that appeal to you.

2. *Body of the Letter.* The body of the cover letter should show the employer that you have researched the company and the position. Using the information from your research, describe your skills, experience, and special attributes as they relate to the needs of the company and describe how you can be an asset to the company. The prospective employer will want to know why he or she should hire you. Share with the employer your goals as they relate to the employer's goals or mission, your knowledge of their productions, and your knowledge about the industry as a whole.

3. *Refer the reader your resume.* Do not restate your resume, but point out some highlights of immediate interest to the reader.

4. *Conclusion.* In the closing paragraph of the cover letter, specify a date when you will contact the employer to confirm receipt of your resume and discuss what opportunities might be available to you. Many individuals leave it up to the employer to make the initial contact, however this can be viewed as a passive attitude. If an employer requests that you do not call, you need to respect that request. Remember, you want to be assertive, not aggressive.

DO	DON'T
Address the cover letter to an individual. "To Whom It May Concern" is not as personal as a name.	Use a form letter for every application. You should tailor it to the job description and the company.
Call to find out the name and title of the individual who will be accepting resumes.	If the company requests no phone calls, do not call. Sometimes, however, addressing the letter "To Whom It May Concern" or to the Personnel Manager is unavoidable.
Keep it brief but thorough.	Repeat your resume. Rather, expand on one or two things in your resume that the employer would find impressive.
Make sure the final copy is professional. Use quality paper, use a business letter format, and sign the letter.	Make any mistakes. Make sure you check grammar, spelling, and punctuation whether you apply via mail or online.

Sample Cover Letter

A sample cover letter follows.

Jayne Witkowski
1500 North Patterson
Valdosta, GA 31698
(229) 555-1212

March 9, 2009

Tim Rollenhagen
News Director
WZZ Television
1100 Main Street
Atlanta, GA 30033

Dear Mr. Rollenhagen:

I am interested in applying for your videographer position recently advertised on your news website. The skills that I have from my work experience, coupled with my academic background, have given me the training necessary to excel in this field.

As you can see from my resume, I recently completed an internship with WWR-TV5 in Savannah. Through my internship, I had the opportunity to receive training in field shooting, non-linear editing, and setting up remote live feeds.

I have also had the opportunity to work at my University's television channel, VSU-TV11. In this capacity, I have served as a field videographer on DVC-Pro equipment for our award-winning student newscasts.

I appreciate your review of my application materials. I look forward to meeting with you to discuss my skills and experiences.

Sincerely,

Jayne Witkowski

Enclosure

Writing Samples

Now more than ever, potential employers are requesting writing samples from applicants. These range from news reporters to public relations specialists. A few technical positions do not require professional writing samples, but with the increasingly competitive job market, candidates may need to produce samples as organizations strive to hire the most suitable applicants.

Although writing samples may be requested as part of the initial portfolio for the broacast news field, they are more likely to be requested once a candidate has completed the first interview. All samples must adhere to standard Associated Press style, and many employers will accept samples created from collegiate news courses. Some news directors, however, prefer writing to be done under deadline, and a second interview may be used to test an applicant's writing skills.

For the print media, writing samples are expected as part of the portfolio and are usually obtained from collegiate newspapers or yearbooks. Again, there are occasional editors who will request a live demonstration of writing ability, but most are satisfied with tearsheets of previous work.

Advertising and public relations will require writing samples, usually gleaned from previous campaigns or class projects. The number of samples required is usually listed as part of the job posting.

Submitting the Portfolio

Unless the hiring authority has asked for the portfolio to be delivered the next day, the package can be sent via regular or second day priority mail. An overnight package will not impress anyone at the media outlet. Applicants should never expect portfolio materials to be returned. The inclusion of a self-addressed, stamped envelope is no guarantee that the material will be returned. The postage for return may be more than the value of the materials. Applicants should plan to make multiple copies before submitting a portfolio and not bother to request the return of materials.

Conclusion

A professional portfolio is vital to a successful job search. Given the amount of competition a job applicant will face, portfolio development must be taken seriously, with a critical assessment of past work and a clear understanding of what a potential employer requires. Applicants should follow the recommended guidelines presented in this chapter for preparing and submitting portfolios. It should be noted that applicants should thoroughly review the employment advertisements before submission, since specifications for desired portfolios may vary among employers.

REFERENCES

The Valdosta State University Career Services Center provided the templates and advice tables for the cover letter and resume construction portions of this chapter.
Graduating seniors within Valdosta State University's Mass Media program, with only their names and contact information changed, provided the sample resumes.

State Resources

This state-by-state guide of resources includes state broadcasting associations, state film commissions, and collegiate programs in Journalism, Communications, and Mass Communications. Additionally, each state's television markets are listed by market size, from New York City (1) to Glendive, Montana (210). The market information is courtesy of The Nielsen Company's *Local Television Market Universe Estimates, 2008.*

Alabama

State Broadcasting Association: al-ba.com
State Film Commission: alabamafilm.org
Media Markets—Birmingham (40), Mobile (62), Huntsville (84), Montgomery (116), Dothan (172)

Media Programs

University	City	Department / School
Alabama State University	Montgomery	Communications
Auburn University	Auburn	Communication and Journalism
Jacksonville State University	Jacksonville	Communication
Miles College	Fairfield	Communications
Samford University	Birmingham	Journalism and Mass Communications
Troy University	Troy	Hall School of Journalism
University of Alabama	Tuscaloosa	Telecommunication and Film or Communication and Information Sciences
University of South Alabama	Mobile	Communication

Alaska

State Broadcasting Association: akbroadcasters.org
State Film Commission: alaskafilm.org
Media Markets—Anchorage (155), Fairbanks (203), Juneau (207)

Media Programs

University	City	Department / School
University of Alaska, Anchorage	Anchorage	Journalism and Public Communications
University of Alaska, Fairbanks	Fairbanks	Journalism

Arizona

State Broadcasting Association: Azbroadcasters.org
State Film Commission: azcommerce.com/film
Media Markets—Phoenix (14), Tucson (71), Yuma (170)

Media Programs

University	City	Department / School
Arizona State University	Phoenix	Walter Cronkite School of Journalism and Mass Communication
Northern Arizona University	Flagstaff	Communication
University of Arizona	Tucson	Journalism

Arkansas

State Broadcasting Association: arkbroadcasters.org
No state film website listed
Media Markets—Little Rock (57), Fort Smith (104), Jonesboro (179)

Media Programs

University	City	Department / School
Arkansas State University	State University	Journalism
Arkansas Tech University	Russellville	Speech, Theatre and Journalism
Harding University	Searcy	Communication
Henderson State University	Arkadelphia	Communication and Theatre Arts
John Brown University	Siloam Springs	Communication
University of Arkansas, Fayetteville	Fayetteville	Walter J. Lemke Department of Journalism
University of Arkansas, Little Rock	Little Rock	Journalism
University of Central Arkansas	Conway	Mass Communication and Theater
University of the Ozarks	Clarksville	Communications

California

State Broadcasting Association: yourcba.com
State Film Commission: film.ca.gov
Media Markets—Los Angeles (2), San Francisco (6), Sacramento (19), San Diego (26), Fresno (56), Santa Barbara (122), Monterey (125), Bakersfield (128), Chico (130), Palm Springs (153), Eureka (194)

Media Programs

University	City	Department / School
American Inter-Continental University	Los Angeles	Media Production
Azusa Pacific University	Azusa	Communication Studies
California Lutheran University	Thousand Oaks	Communication

(continued)

University	City	Department / School
California Polytechnic State University	San Luis Obispo	Journalism
California State Polytechnic, Pomona	Pomona	Communication
California State University, Chico	Chico	Communication Design or Journalism
California State University, Dominguez Hills	Carson	Communications
California State University, East Bay	Hayward	Communication
California State University, Fresno	Fresno	Mass Communication and Journalism
California State University, Fullerton	Fullerton	Communications
California State University, Long Beach	Long Beach	Journalism
California State University, Los Angeles	Los Angeles	Communication Studies
California State University, Northridge	Northridge	Cinema and Television Arts or Journalism
California State University, Sacramento	Sacramento	Communication Studies
City College of San Francisco	San Francisco	Broadcast Electronic Media Arts
College of San Mateo	San Mateo	Broadcast & Electronic Media
Golden West College	Huntington Beach	Broadcast and Video Production
Grossmont Community College	El Cajon	Media Communications
Humboldt State University	Arcata	Journalism & Mass Communication
Long Beach City College	Long Beach	Music, Radio & Television
Loyola Marymount University	Los Angeles	Film and Television
Menlo College	Atherton	Mass Communications
Mount San Antonio College	Walnut	Broadcasting
Pacific Union College	Angwin	Communication
Palomor College	San Marcos	Communications
Pasadena City College	Pasadena	Communication
Pepperdine University	Malibu	Journalism
Point Loma Nazarene University	San Diego	Communication and Theatre
Saddleback College	Mission Viejo	Communication Arts
Saint Mary's College of California	Moraga	Communication
San Diego State University	San Diego	Communication
San Francisco State University	San Francisco	Broadcast & Electronic Communication Arts or Journalism
San Jose State University	San Jose	Television, Radio, Film, and Theatre or Journalism and Mass Communications

(continued)

University	City	Department / School
Santa Ana College/Santiago Canyon College	Santa Ana	TV/Video Communications
Santa Clara University	Santa Clara	Communication
Stanford University	Stanford	Communication
University of California, Berkeley	Berkeley	Graduate School of Journalism
University of La Verne	La Verne	Communications
University of San Francisco	San Francisco	Communication Studies
University of Southern California	Los Angeles	Annenberg School for Communication
University of the Pacific	Stockton	Communication

Colorado

State Broadcasting Association: http://e-cba.org
State Film Commission: coloradofilm.org
Media Markets — Denver (18), Colorado Springs (93), Grand Junction (187)

Media Programs

University	City	Department / School
Adams State College	Alamosa	Communications
Aims Community College	Greeley	Communications Media
Colorado State University	Fort Collins	Journalism and Technical Communication
Mesa State College	Grand Junction	Mass Communications
Metropolitan State College of Denver	Denver	Communication Arts & Sciences
University of Colorado	Boulder	Journalism & Mass Communication
University of Denver	Denver	Communication
University of North Colorado	Greeley	Journalism and Mass Communications

Connecticut

State Broadcasting Association: ctba.org
State Film Commission: ctfilm.com
Media Markets—Hartford (28)

Media Programs

University	City	Department / School
Eastern Connecticut State University	Willimantic	Communication
Quinnipiac University	Hamden	Communications

(continued)

University	City	Department / School
Southern Connecticut State University	New Haven	Communication, Information and Library Science
University of Bridgeport	Bridgeport	Mass Communications
University of Connecticut	Storrs	Journalism
University of Hartford	West Hartford	Communication

Delaware

State Broadcasting Association: mdcd.com
State Film Commission: http://dedo.delaware.gov/filmoffice
Media Markets—The entire state of Delaware is part of the Philadelphia, Pennsylvania, television market. There are, however, stations in Dover and Wilmington.

Media Programs

University	City	Department / School
Delaware State University	Dover	Mass Communications
University of Delaware	Newark	Communication

District Of Columbia

State Broadcasting Association: mdcd.com
State Film Commission: film.dc.gov
Media Markets—Washington, DC (8)

Media Programs

University	City	Department / School
American University	Washington	Communication
George Washington University	Washington	Media and Public Affairs
Georgetown University	Washington	Communication, Culture and Technology
Howard University	Washington	The John H. Johnson School of Communications

Florida

State Broadcasting Association: fab.org
State Film Commission: filminflorida.com
Media Markets—Tampa (12), Miami (17), Orlando (20), West Palm Beach (38), Jacksonville (52), Fort Myers (66), Tallahassee (109), Palm Springs (153), Panama City (157), Gainesville (162)

Media Programs

University	City	Department / School
Art Institute of Fort Lauderdale	Fort Lauderdale	Media Arts
Barry University	Miami Shores	Communication
City College	Fort Lauderdale	Broadcasting

(continued)

University	City	Department / School
Edward Waters College	Jacksonville	Mass Communications
Flagler College	Saint Augustine	Communication
Florida A&M	Tallahassee	Journalism and Graphic Communication
Florida International University	North Miami	Journalism & Mass Communication
Florida Southern College	Lakeland	Communication
Florida State University	Tallahassee	Communications
Hillsborough Community College	Tampa	Radio & Television Broadcast Program
Jacksonville University	Jacksonville	Communication
University of Central Florida	Orlando	Nicholson School of Communication
University of Florida	Gainesville	Journalism and Communications
University of Miami	Coral Gables	Communication
University of South Florida	Tampa	Mass Communications
University of South Florida, St. Petersburg	St. Petersburg	Journalism and Media Studies
University of West Florida	Pensacola	Communication Arts

Georgia

State Broadcasting Association: gab.org
State Film Commission: georgia.org/EntertainmentIndustry/FilmAndVideo
Media Markets—Atlanta (9), Savannah (97), Augusta (115), Macon (120), Columbus (127), Albany (147)

Media Programs

University	City	Department / School
Berry College	Mount Berry	Communication
Brenau University	Gainesville	Mass Communication
Clark Atlanta University	Atlanta	Mass Media Arts
Emory University	Atlanta	Journalism
Georgia Southern University	Statesboro	Communication Arts
Georgia State University	Atlanta	Communication
Mercer University	Macon	Communication and Theatre Arts
Savannah College of Art and Design	Savannah	Broadcast Design & Motion Graphics
Savannah State University	Savannah	Mass Communications
Toccoa Falls College	Toccoa Falls	Communication
University of Georgia	Athens	H.W. Grady College of Journalism and Mass Communication
Valdosta State University	Valdosta	Communication Arts

Hawaii

State Broadcasting Association: hawaiibroadcasters.com
State Film Commission: hawaiifilmoffice.com
Media Markets—Honolulu (72)

Media Programs

University	City	Department / School
Chaminade University Of Honolulu	Honolulu	Communication
Hawaii Pacific University	Honolulu	Communication
University Of Hawaii At Mānoa	Honolulu	Communications

Idaho

State Broadcasting Association: idahobroadcasters.org
State Film Commission: filmidaho.com
Media Markets—Boise (119), Idaho Falls (163), Twin Falls (192)

Media Programs

University	City	Department / School
Boise State University	Boise	Communication
South Suburban College	South Holland	Communications & Humanities
University of Idaho	Moscow	Journalism & Mass Media

Illinois

State Broadcasting Association: ilba.org
State Film Commission: illinoisbiz.biz/film
Media Markets—Chicago (3), Champaign (82), Peoria (117), Quincy (169)

Media Programs

University	City	Department / School
Bradley University	Peoria	Slane College of Communications and Fine Arts
College of St. Francis	Joliet	Mass Communication
Columbia College Chicago	Chicago	Journalism
DePaul University	Chicago	Communication Arts and Sciences
Eastern Illinois University	Charleston	Journalism
Illinois College	Jacksonville	Communications and Theatre
Illinois State University	Normal	Communication
Loyola University of Chicago	Chicago	Communication
MacMurray College	Jacksonville	Journalism
North Central College	Naperville	Speech Communication
Northern Illinois University	De Kalb	Communication
Northwestern University	Evanston	Medill School of Journalism

(continued)

University	City	Department / School
Principia College	Elsah	Mass Communication
Roosevelt University	Chicago	Communication
Saint Xavier University	Chicago	Mass Communications
Southern Illinois University, Carbondale	Carbondale	Journalism
Southern Illinois University, Edwardsville	Edwardsville	Mass Communications
University of Illinois, Urbana-Champaign	Champaign	Communications
University of St. Francis	Joliet	Mass Communication
Western Illinois University	Macomb	English and Journalism

Indiana

State Broadcasting Association: indianabroadcasters.org
State Film Commission: in.gov/film
Media Markets—Indianapolis (25), South Bend (87), Evansville (100), Fort Wayne (106), Terre Haute (150), Lafayette (191)

Media Programs

University	City	Department / School
Anderson University	Anderson	Communication
Ball State University	Muncie	Journalism or Telecommunications
Butler University	Indianapolis	Eugene S. Pulliam School of Journalism
Calumet College of St. Joseph	Whiting	English and Professional Writing
DePauw University	Greencastle	Communication and Theatre
Goshen College	Goshen	Communication
Indiana State University	Terre Haute	Communication
Indiana University	Bloomington	Telecommunications or Journalism
Manchester College	North Manchester	Communication Studies
Purdue University, Calumet	Hammond	Communication
Saint Mary-of-the-Woods College	Saint Mary-of-the-Woods	English, Journalism and Languages
Taylor University, Fort Wayne Campus	Fort Wayne	Communication Arts
University of Evansville	Evansville	Communication
University of Indianapolis	Indianapolis	Communication
University of Notre Dame	Notre Dame	Film, Television, and Theatre
University of Southern Indiana	Evansville	Communications
Valparaiso University	Valparaiso	Communication
Vincennes University	Vincennes	Journalism

Iowa

State Broadcasting Association: iowabroadcasters.com
State Film Commission: traveliowa.com/film/
Media Markets—Des Moines (73), Cedar Rapids (88), Davenport (95), Sioux City (143),
   Ottumwa (199)

Media Programs

University	City	Department / School
Briar Cliff University	Sioux City	Mass Media
Buena Vista University	Storm Lake	Media Studies
Clarke College	Dubuque	Communication
Drake University	Des Moines	Journalism and Mass Communication
Grand View College	Des Moines	Communication
Iowa Lakes Community College	Estherville	Broadcast Media
Iowa State University	Ames	Greenlee School of Journalism and Communication
Northwest Iowa Community College	Sheldon	Journalism – Pre Professional
St. Ambrose University	Davenport	Communication
University of Iowa	Iowa City	Journalism & Mass Communication
University of Northern Iowa	Cedar Falls	Communication Studies
Wartburg College	Waverly	Communication Arts

Kansas

State Broadcasting Association: kab.net
State Film Commission: http://kdoch.state.ks.us/kdfilm/index.jsp
Media Markets—Wichita (67), Topeka (136)

Media Programs

University	City	Department / School
Baker University	Baldwin City	Communication and Theatre Arts
Fort Hays State University	Hays	Communication Studies
Johnson County Community College	Overland Park	Journalism and Mass Communications
Kansas State University	Manhattan	A.Q. Miller School of Journalism & Mass Communications
Pittsburg State University	Pittsburg	Communication
University of Kansas	Lawrence	William Allen White School of Journalism and Mass Communications
Washburn University	Topeka	Mass Media
Wichita State University	Wichita State	Elliott School of Communication

Kentucky

State Broadcasting Association: kba.org
State Film Commission: kyfilmoffice.com
Media Markets—Louisville (50), Lexington (63), Paducah (80)

Media Programs

University	City	Department / School
Asbury College	Wilmore	Communication Arts
Eastern Kentucky University	Richmond	Communication
Morehead State University	Morehead	Communication and Theatre
Murray State University	Murray	Journalism and Mass Communications
National College of Business & Technology	Lexington	Radio & Television Broadcasting
Northern Kentucky University	Highland Heights	Communication
University of Kentucky	Lexington	Journalism and Telecommunications
University of Louisville	Louisville	Communications
Western Kentucky University	Bowling Green	Journalism and Broadcasting

Louisiana

State Broadcasting Association: broadcasters.org
State Film Commission: lafilm.org
Media Markets—New Orleans (43), Shreveport (81), Baton Rouge (96), Lafayette (124), Lake Charles (175), Alexandria (176)

Media Programs

University	City	Department / School
Bossier Parish Community College	Bossier City	Telecommunications
Grambling State University	Grambling	Mass Communication
Louisiana College	Pineville	Communication Arts
Louisiana State University, Baton Rouge	Baton Rouge	Manship School of Mass Communication
Louisiana State University, Shreveport	Shreveport	Communications
Louisiana Tech University, Ruston	Ruston	Journalism
Loyola University	New Orleans	Mass Communication
McNeese State University	Lake Charles	Mass Communication
Northwestern State University	Natchitoches	Journalism
Nicholls State University	Thibodaux	Mass Communication
Southeastern State University of Louisiana	Hammond	Communication
Southern University	Baton Rouge	Mass Communications

(continued)

University	City	Department / School
Tulane University	New Orleans	Communication
University of Louisiana, Lafayette	Lafayette	Communication
University of Louisiana, Monroe	Monroe	Communication
University of New Orleans	New Orleans	Film, Theatre & Communication Arts
Xavier University of Louisiana	New Orleans	Communications

Maine

State Broadcasting Association: mab.org
State Film Commission: filminmaine.com
Media Markets—Portland (74), Bangor (151), Presque Isle (204)

Media Programs

University	City	Department / School
Howard Community College	Columbia	Arts & Humanities – Mass Media
Husson College	Bangor	New England School of Communication
University of Maine	Orono	Communication & Journalism

Maryland

State Broadcasting Association: mdcd.com
State Film Commission: marylandfilm.org
Media Markets—Baltimore (24), Salisbury (148)

Media Programs

University	City	Department / School
Bowie State University	Bowie	Communications
Columbia Union College	Takoma Park	Communication and Journalism
Defense Information School	Fort George G. Meade	Journalism
Hood College	Frederick	English and Communication Arts
Loyola College	Baltimore	Communication
Montgomery College	Rockville	Communication Arts Technologies
Morgan State University	Baltimore	Communication Studies
Prince George's Community College	Largo	Communication Theatre
Salisbury University	Salisbury	Communication and Theatre Arts
Towson University	Towson	Mass Communication and Communication Studies
University of Maryland, College Park	College Park	Philip Merrill College of Journalism

Massachusetts

State Broadcasting Association: massbroadcasters.org
State Film Commission: None listed
Media Markets—Boston (5), Springfield (108)

Media Programs

University	City	Department / School
Boston University	Boston	Communication
Emerson College	Boston	Journalism
Harvard University	Cambridge	Nieman Program
Mount Wachusett Community College	Gardner	Broadcasting and Telecommunications
Northeastern University	Boston	Journalism
Simmons College	Boston	Communications
Stonehill College	Easton	Communication
Suffolk University	Boston	Communication and Journalism
University of Massachusetts, Amherst	Amherst	Journalism

Michigan

State Broadcasting Association: michmab.com
State Film Commission: michigan.gov/filmoffice
Media Markets—Detroit (11), Grand Rapids (39), Flint (65), Lansing (110), Traverse City (113), Marquette (180), Alpena (208)

Media Programs

University	City	Department / School
Alma College	Alma	Communication
Calvin College	Grand Rapids	Communication Arts and Sciences
Central Michigan University	Mt. Pleasant	Broadcast & Cinematic Arts or Journalism
Eastern Michigan University	Ypsilanti	Communication and Theatre Arts
Ferris State University	Big Rapids	Television and Digital Media Production
Grand Valley State University	Allendale	Communications
Henry Ford Community College	Dearborn	Telecommunication
Lansing Community College	East Lansing	Media Technologies
Madonna University	Livonia	Journalism, Public Relations
Michigan State University	East Lansing	Telecommunication, Information Studies and Media or Journalism
Oakland University	Rochester	Rhetoric, Communication and Journalism
Spring Arbor University	Spring Arbor	Communication

(continued)

University	City	Department / School
University of Detroit Mercy	Detroit	Communication Studies
University of Michigan	Ann Arbor	Communications Studies
Washtenaw Community College	Ann Arbor	Digital Video / Film Technology
Wayne State University	Detroit	Communication
Western Michigan University	Kalamazoo	Communication

Minnesota

State Broadcasting Association: minnesotabroadcasters.com
State Film Commission: mnfilmtv.org
Media Markets—Minneapolis (15), Duluth (137), Rochester (152), Mankato (200)

Media Programs

University	City	Department / School
Bemidji State University	Bemidji	Mass Communication
Brown College	Mendota Heights	Radio Broadcasting
Hamline University	St. Paul	Communication Studies
Mankato State University	Mankato	Mass Communications
Moorhead State University	Moorhead	Mass Communications
Normandale Community College	Minneapolis	Mass Communications
Northwestern College	St. Paul	Communication Studies
St. Cloud State University	St. Cloud	Mass Communications
St. Mary's University	Winona	Media Communications
University of Minnesota	Minneapolis	Journalism and Mass Communication
University of St. Thomas	St. Paul	Journalism and Mass Communication
Winona State University	Winona	Mass Communication

Mississippi

State Broadcasting Association: msbroadcasters.org
State Film Commission: visitmississippi.org/film
Media Markets—Jackson (89), Columbus (132), Biloxi (158), Hattiesburg (167)

Media Programs

University	City	Department / School
Alcorn State University	Lorman	Communications
Jackson State University	Jackson	Mass Communications
Meridian Community College	Meridian	Broadcast Communication Technology

(continued)

University	City	Department / School
Mississippi State University	Mississippi State	Communication
Mississippi University for Women	Columbus	Business and Communication
Mississippi Valley State University	Itta Bena	Mass Communications
Rust College	Holly Springs	Mass Communications
Tougaloo College	Jackson	Journalism
University of Mississippi	University	Journalism
University of Southern Mississippi	Hattiesburg	Mass Communication & Journalism

Missouri

State Broadcasting Association: mbaweb.org
State Film Commission: showmemissouri.org/film
Media Markets—St. Louis (21), Kansas City (31), Springfield (77), Columbia (138), Joplin (145), St. Joseph (201)

Media Programs

University	City	Department / School
Central Missouri State University	Warrensburg	Communication
Culver-Stockton College	Canton	Communication
Evangel University	Springfield	Communication
Lincoln University	Jefferson City	Humanities, Fine Arts and Journalism
Lindenwood University	St. Charles	Communications
Missouri Southern State University	Joplin	Communication
Missouri State University	Springfield	Communication Studies
Missouri Western State College	St. Joseph	English, Foreign Languages and Journalism
Northwest Missouri State University	Maryville	Mass Communication
Southeast Missouri State University	Cape Girardeau	Communication
St. Louis University	St. Louis	Communication
Stephens College	Columbia	Mass Media
Truman State University	Kirksville	Communication
University of Missouri, Columbia	Columbia	Journalism
University of Missouri, Kansas City	Kansas City	Communication Studies
University of Missouri, St. Louis	St. Louis	Communication
Webster University	St. Louis	Communications

Montana

State Broadcasting Association: mtbroadcasters.org
State Film Commission: montanafilm.com
Media Markets—Missoula (168), Billings (171), Great Falls (189), Butte (193), Helena (206), Glendive (210)

Media Programs

University	City	Department / School
University of Montana	Missoula	Journalism

Nebraska

State Broadcasting Association: ne-ba.org
State Film Commission: filmnebraska.com
Media Markets—Omaha (75), Lincoln (103), North Platte (209)

Media Programs

University	City	Department / School
Creighton University	Omaha	Journalism and Mass Communication
Doane College	Crete	Communications
Hastings College	Hastings	Communication Arts, Business and Economics
University of Nebraska, Kearney	Kearney	Communications
University of Nebraska, Lincoln	Lincoln	Journalism and Mass Communications
University of Nebraska, Omaha	Omaha	Communication
Wayne State College	Wayne	Communication Arts

Nevada

State Broadcasting Association: nevadabroadcasters.org
State Film Commission: nevadafilm.com
Media Markets—Law Vegas (48), Reno (112)

Media Programs

University	City	Department / School
University of Nevada, Las Vegas	Las Vegas	Greenspun School of Communication
University of Nevada, Reno	Reno	Donald W. Reynolds School of Journalism

New Hampshire

State Broadcasting Association: nhab.org
State Film Commission: filmnh.org/commission.htm
Media Markets—The entire state of New Hampshire is part of the Boston, Massachusetts, television market. There are, however, stations in Derry and Manchester.

Media Programs

University	City	Department / School
Keene State College	Keene	Communication
University of New Hampshire	Manchester	Communication

New Jersey

State Broadcasting Association: njba.com
State Film Commission: njfilm.org
Media Markets—The entire state of New Jersey is predominantly within the New York City and Philadelphia, Pennsylvania, markets. There are, however, stations in Atlantic City, Camden, East Orange, Newark and Trenton.

Media Programs

University	City	Department / School
Bergen Community College	Paramus	Media Technologies
Camden County College	Blackwood	Communications
County College of Morris	Randolph	Visual Arts
Fairleigh Dickinson University	Teaneck	Communication Studies
Mercer County Community College	West Windsor	Radio – TV Program
Monmouth University	West Long Branch	Communication
Montclair State University	Montclair	Broadcasting
Rider University	Lawrenceville	Communication
Rowan University	Glassboro	Communication
Rutgers University	New Brunswick	Communication, Information Technologies & Journalism
Seton Hall University	South Orange	Communication
William Paterson University	Wayne	Communication

New Mexico

State Broadcasting Association: newmexicorbroadcasters.org
State Film Commission: edd.state.nm.us/film
Media Markets—Albuquerque (46)

Media Programs

University	City	Department / School
Eastern New Mexico University	Portales	Communicative Arts and Sciences
New Mexico Highlands University	Las Vegas	Mass Communication
New Mexico State University	Las Cruces	Journalism and Mass Communications
University of New Mexico	Albuquerque	Communication and Journalism

New York

State Broadcasting Association: nysbroadcastersassn.org
State Film Commission: nylovesfilm.com
Media Markets—New York (1), Buffalo (49), Albany (55), Syracuse (76), Rochester (79), Binghamton (156), Utica (166), Elmira (173)

Media Programs

University	City	Department / School
Brooklyn College of the City University of New York	Brooklyn	Television and Radio
Buffalo State College	Buffalo	Communication
Canisius College	Buffalo	Digital Media Arts
Cayuga Community College	Auburn	Telecommunications/Broadcasting
Columbia University	New York	Graduate School of Journalism
Cornell University	Ithaca	Communication
Finger Lakes Community College	Canandaigua	Visual and Performance Arts
Fordham University	Bronx	Communication and Media Studies
Hofstra University	Hempstead	Journalism, Media Studies and Public Relations
Hudson Valley Community College	Troy	Broadcast Communications
Iona College	New Rochelle	Mass Communication
Ithaca College	Ithaca	Roy H. Park School of Communications
Kingsborough Community College	Brooklyn	Communications & Performing Arts
Long Island University, Brooklyn	Brooklyn	Journalism
Long Island University, Southhampton	Brookville	Arts & Media
Marist College	Poughkeepsie	Communication and the Arts
New York University	New York	Journalism or Tisch School of the Arts
Niagara University	Niagara University	Communication Studies
Onondaga Community College	Syracuse	Telecommunications Tech Program
Pace University	New York City	Communications
Rochester Institute of Technology	Rochester	Film / Video / Animation or Digital Cinema
Southampton College	Southampton	Graduate Campus

(continued)

University	City	Department / School
St. Bonaventure University	Saint Bonaventure	Russell J. Jandoli School of Journalism and Mass Communication
St. John Fisher College	Rochester	Communication / Journalism
St. John's University	Queens	Mass Communications, Journalism, Television and Film
Stony Brook	Stony Brook	Media Arts
SUNY, Albany	Albany	Communication
SUNY, Brockport	Brockport	Communication
SUNY, Buffalo	Buffalo	Communication
SUNY, Fredonia	Fredonia	Communication
SUNY, Morrisville	Morrisville	Journalism at Morrisville State College
SUNY, Oswego	Oswego	Communication Studies
SUNY, New Paltz	New Paltz	Communication and Media
SUNY, Plattsburgh	Plattsburgh	Communication Program
Syracuse University	Syracuse	S.I. Newhouse School of Public Communications
Utica College	Utica	Journalism

North Carolina

State Broadcasting Association: ncbroadcast.com
State Film Commission: ncfilm.com
Media Markets—Charlotte (27), Raleigh (29), Greensboro (47), Greenville (105), Wilmington (139)

Media Programs

University	City	Department / School
Appalachian State University	Boone	Communication
Campbell University	Buies Creek	Mass Communication
East Carolina University	Greenville	Communication
Elon University	Elon	Communications
Gardner, Webb University	Boiling Springs	Communication Studies
Isothermal Community College	Spindale	Broadcasting Production Technology
Johnson C. Smith University	Charlotte	Communication
Lenior-Rhyne College	Hickory	Arts, Theatre Arts and Communication
North Carolina A&T State University	Greensboro	Journalism and Mass Communication
University of North Carolina, Asheville	Asheville	Mass Communication
University of North Carolina, Chapel Hill	Chapel Hill	Journalism and Mass Communication

(continued)

University	City	Department / School
University of North Carolina, Greensboro	Greensboro	Broadcasting and Cinema
University of North Carolina, Pembroke	Pembroke	Mass Communication
University of North Carolina, Wilmington	Wilmington	Communication Studies
Wake Forest University	Winston Salem	Communication
Wingate University	Wingate	Communication Studies

North Dakota

State Broadcasting Association: ndba.org
State Film Commission: ndtourism.com
Media Markets—Fargo (118), Minot (160)

Media Programs

University	City	Department / School
North Dakota State University	Fargo	Communication
University of North Dakota	Grand Forks	Communication

Ohio

State Broadcasting Association – oab.org
State Film Commission: ohiofilm.com
Media Markets—Cleveland (16), Columbus (32), Cincinnati (34), Toledo (70), Youngstown (102), Bowling Green (183), Lima (185), Zanesville (202)

Media Programs

University	City	Department / School
Ashland University	Ashland	Communication Arts, Electronic Media Production
Bowling Green State University	Bowling Green	Journalism
Cedarville College	Cedarville	Communication Arts
Cleveland State University	Cleveland	Communication
Franciscan University of Steubenville	Steubenville	Communication Arts
International College of Broadcasting	Dayton	Radio & Television
John Carroll University	University Heights	Communications

(continued)

University	City	Department / School
Kent State University	Kent	Journalism and Mass Communication
Lorain County Community College	Elyria	Communications and Creative Arts
Marietta College	Marietta	Mass Media
Miami University	Oxford	Communications
Muskingum College	New Concord	Journalism
Northern Ohio University	Ada	Communication Arts, Broadcasting & Electronic Media
Ohio State University	Columbus	Communication
Ohio University	Athens	E.W. Scripps School of Journalism
Ohio Wesleyan University	Delaware	Journalism
Otterbein College	Westerville	Communication
University of Akron	Akron	Communication
University of Cincinnati	Cincinnati	Electronic Media
University of Dayton	Dayton	Communication
University of Toledo	Toledo	Communication
Washington State Community College	Marietta	Mass Media Broadcasting
Wright State University	Dayton	Communication
Xavier University	Cincinnati	Communication Arts
Youngstown State University	Youngstown	English

Oklahoma

State Broadcasting Association: oabok.org
State Film Commission: oklahomafilm.org
Media Markets—Oklahoma City (45), Dayton (59), Tulsa (61)

Media Programs

University	City	Department / School
Cameron University	Lawton	Communications
East Central University	Ada	Communication
Langston University	Langston	Communication and English
Northeastern State University	Talequah	Communication and Theatre
Northern Oklahoma College	Stillwater	Broadcasting and Communications
Northwestern Oklahoma State University	Alva	Mass Communications
Oklahoma Baptist University	Shawnee	Journalism and Public Relations
Oklahoma Christian University	Oklahoma City	Communication

(continued)

University	City	Department / School
Oklahoma City Community College	Oklahoma City	Communications
Oklahoma City University	Oklahoma City	Mass Communications
Oklahoma State University	Stillwater	Paul Miller School of Journalism and Broadcasting
Oral Roberts University	Tulsa	Communication Arts
Rogers State University	Claremore	Communications & Fine Arts
Rose State University	Midwest City	Broadcast Production & Technology
Southeastern Oklahoma State University	Durant	Communications & Theatre
Southern Nazarene University	Bethany	Mass Communication / Journalism
University of Central Oklahoma	Edmond	Mass Communication
University of Oklahoma	Norman	Gaylord College of Journalism and Mass Communication
University of Tulsa	Tulsa	Communication

Oregon

State Broadcasting Association: theoab.org
State Film Commission: oregonfilm.org
Media Markets—Portland (23), Eugene (121), Medford (141), Bend (196)

Media Programs

University	City	Department / School
Linfield College	McMinnville	Theatre and Communication Arts
Southern Oregon University	Ashland	Communication
University of Oregon	Eugene	Journalism and Communication
University of Portland	Portland	Communication Studies

Pennsylvania

State Broadcasting Association: pab.org
State Film Commission: filminpa.com
Media Markets—Philadelphia (4), Pittsburgh (22), Harrisburg (41), Wilkes Barre (54), Johnstown (98), Erie (142)

Media Programs

University	City	Department / School
Allegheny College	Meadville	Communication Arts
Bloomsburg University	Bloomsburg	Mass Communications
Cabrini College	Radnor	English and Communications
California University of Pennsylvania	California	Student Association, Inc.

(continued)

University	City	Department / School
Clarion University	Clarion	Communication
College Misericordia	Dallas	Communications
Drexel University	Drexel University	Media Arts & Design
Duquesne University	Pittsburgh	Communication & Rhetorical Studies
Elizabethtown College	Elizabethtown	Communications
Indiana University of Pennsylvania	Indiana	Communications Media
Kutztown University	Kutztown	Electronic Media
La Salle University	Philadelphia	Communication
Lehigh University	Bethlehem	Journalism and Communication
Lock Haven University	Lock Haven	Journalism and Mass Communication
Lycoming College	Williamsport	Communication
Millersville University	Millersville	Communication and Theatre
Pennsylvania State University	University Park	Communications
Point Park University	Pittsburgh	Journalism and Mass Communication
Robert Morris University	Moon Township	Media Arts
Shippensburg University	Shippensburg	Communication/Journalism
Slippery Rock University	Slippery Rock	Communication
Susquehanna University	Selinsgrove	Communications and Theatre
Temple University	Philadelphia	Communications and Theater
University of Pennsylvania	Philadephia	Annenberg School for Communication
University of Pittsburgh	Pittsburgh	Communication
University of Scranton	Scranton	Communication
Ursinus College	Collegeville	Media and Communication Studies
Westminster College	New Wilmington	Communication Studies, Theatre, and Art
Wilkes University	Wilkes-Barre	Communication Studies
York College of Pennsylvania	York	Communications

Rhode Island

State Broadcasting Association: ribroadcasters.com
State Film Commission: film.ri.gov
Media Markets—Providence (51)

Media Programs

University	City	Department / School
New England Institute of Technology	Warwick	Video and Radio Production Technology
University of Rhode Island	Kingston	Journalism

South Carolina

State Broadcasting Association: scba.net
State Film Commission: scfilmoffice.com
Media Markets—Greenville (35), Columbia (83), Charleston (101), Myrtle Beach (107)

Media Programs

University	City	Department / School
Benedict College	Columbia	English, Foreign Language / Mass Communications
Bob Jones University	Greenville	Radio & Television
College of Charleston	Charleston	Communication
Francis Marion University	Florence	Mass Communication
University of South Carolina, Aiken	Aiken	Communications
University of South Carolina, Columbia	Columbia	Journalism and Mass Communication
Winthrop University	Rock Hill	Mass Communication

South Dakota

State Broadcasting Association: sdba.org
State Film Commission: filmsd.com
Media Markets—Sioux Falls (114), Rapid City (177), Watertown (178)

Media Programs

University	City	Department / School
Augustana College	Sioux Falls	Journalism
Black Hills State University	Spearfish	Mass Communication
South Dakota State University	Brookings	Journalism and Mass Communication
University of South Dakota	Vermillion	Contemporary Media and Journalism

Tennessee

State Broadcasting Association: tabtn.org
State Film Commission: tennessee.gov/film/
Media Markets—Nashville (30), Memphis (44), Knoxville (58), Chattanooga (86), Tri-Cities (91), Jackson (174)

Media Programs

University	City	Department / School
Austin Peay State University	Clarksville	Communication and Theatre
Belmont University	Nashville	Media Studies
Carson-Newman College	Jefferson City	Communication

(continued)

University	City	Department / School
Christian Brothers University	Memphis	Communication and Performing Arts
East Tennessee State University	Johnson City	Communication
Middle Tennessee State University	Murfreesboro	Mass Communication
Tennessee Technological University	Cookeville	English—Journalism
University of Memphis	Memphis	Journalism
University of Tennessee, Chattanooga	Chattanooga	Communication
University of Tennessee, Knoxville	Knoxville	Communication and Information
University of Tennessee, Martin	Martin	Communications

Texas

State Broadcasting Association: tab.org
State Film Commission: governor.state.tx.us/film
Media Markets—Dallas (7), Houston (10), San Antonio (37), Austin (53), Harlingen (92),
   Waco (94), El Paso (99), Tyler (111), Corpus Christi (129), Amarillo (131), Beaumont
   (140), Wichita Falls (144), Lubbock (146), Odessa (159), Sherman (161), Abilene
   (164), Laredo (188), San Angelo (197)

Media Programs

University	City	Department / School
Abilene Christian University	Abilene	Journalism and Mass Communication
Amarillo College	Amarillo	Radio—Television / Journalism
Angelo State University	San Angelo	Communications, Drama and Journalism
Austin Community College	Austin	Radio, Television & Film
Baylor University	Waco	Journalism
Del Mar College	Corpus Christi	Radio & Television
Hardin-Simmons University	Abilene	Communication
Houston Baptist University	Houston	Mass Communications
Houston Community College	Houston	Broadcast Technology
Lamar University	Beaumont	Communication
Midwestern State University	Wichita Falls	Mass Communication
Prairie View A&M University	Prairie View	Language and Communications
Richland College	Dallas	Mass Communications / Journalism
Sam Houston State University	Huntsville	Mass Communication
San Antonio College	San Antonio	Radio, Television & Film
Southern Methodist University	Dallas	Journalism
St. Mary's University	San Antonio	English
Stephen F. Austin State University	Nacogdoches	Communication

(continued)

University	City	Department / School
Texas A&M University, College Station	College Station	Journalism Studies
Texas A&M University, Commerce	Commerce	Journalism / News Editorial
Texas A&M University, Kingsville	Kingsville	Communications and Theatre Arts
Texas Christian University	Fort Worth	Schieffer School of Journalism or College of Communication—Radio, TV, Film
Texas Lutheran University	Seguin	English and Communication Studies
Texas Southern University	Houston	Communications
Texas State University	San Marcos	Journalism and Mass Communication
Texas Tech University	Lubbock	Mass Communications
Texas Wesleyan University	Fort Worth	Mass Communications
Trinity University	San Antonio	Communication
University of Houston	Houston	Communication
University of the Incarnate Word	San Antonio	Communication Arts
University of North Texas	Denton	Radio, Television, and Film or Journalism
University of Texas of the Permian Basin	Odessa	Mass Communication
University of Texas, Arlington	Arlington	Communication
University of Texas, Austin	Austin	Journalism or Radio-TV-Film
University of Texas, El Paso	El Paso	Communication
University of Texas, Pan American	Edinburg	Communication
West Texas A&M University	Canyon	Mass Communications

Utah

State Broadcasting Association: utahbroadcasters.com
State Film Commission: film.utah.gov
Media Markets—Salt Lake City (36)

Media Programs

University	City	Department / School
Brigham Young University	Provo	Communication
Southern Utah University	Cedar City	Communication
University of Utah	Salt Lake City	Communication
Utah State University	Logan	Journalism & Communication
Weber State University	Ogden	Communication

Vermont

State Broadcasting Association: vab.org
State Film Commission: vermontfilm.com
Media Markets—Burlington (90)

Media Programs

University	City	Department / School
Lyndon State College	Lyndonville	Television Studies
Monroe Technology Center	SW, Leesburg	Television Production
St. Michael's College	Colchester	Journalism and Mass Communication

Virginia

State Broadcasting Association: vabonline.com
State Film Commission: filmvirginia.org
Media Markets—Norfolk (42), Richmond (60), Roanoke (68)

Media Programs

University	City	Department / School
Emory and Henry College	Emory	Mass Communications
George Mason University	Fairfax	Film & Media Studies
Hampton University	Hampton	Scripps Howard School of Journalism and Communications
James Madison University	Harrisonburg	Media Arts & Design
Liberty University	Lynchburg	Communication Studies
Lynchburg College	Lynchburg	Communication Studies
Mary Baldwin College	Staunton	Communication
Norfolk State University	Norfolk	Mass Communications and Journalism
Radford University	Radford	Media Studies
Regent University	Virginia Beach	Communication and the Arts
University of Richmond	Richmond	Journalism
Virginia Commonwealth University	Richmond	Mass Communications
Virginia Polytechnic Institute and State University	Blacksburg	Communication
Virginia Union University	Richmond	Communications
Virginia Wesleyan	Norfolk	Communications/Journalism
Virginia Western Community College	Roanoke	Radio—Television Production Technology
Washington And Lee University	Lexington	Journalism And Mass Communications

Washington

State Broadcasting Association: wsab.org
State Film Commission: filmwashington.com
Media Markets—Seattle (13), Spokane (78), Yakima (126)

Media Programs

University	City	Department / School
Bellevue Community College	Bellevue	Communication
Central Washington University	Ellensburg	Communication
Clover Park Technical College	Lakewood	Radio Broadcasting
Eastern Washington University	Cheney	Journalism
Gonzaga University	Spokane	Communication Arts
Green River Community College	Auburn	Journalism
Seattle University	Seattle	Communication / Journalism
University of Washington	Seattle	Communication
Walla Walla College	College Place	Communications
Washington State University	Pullman	Edward R. Murrow School of Communication
Western Washington University	Bellingham	Journalism
Whitworth College	Spokane	Communication Studies

West Virginia

State Broadcasting Association: wvba.com
State Film Commission: wvfilm.com
Media Markets—Charleston (64), Bluefield (149), Wheeling (154), Clarksburg (165)

Media Programs

University	City	Department / School
Bethany College	Bethany	Communication
Marshall University	Huntington	W. Page Pitt School of Journalism and Mass Communications
West Virginia University	Morgantown	Perley Isaac Reed School of Journalism

Wisconsin

State Broadcasting Association: wi-broadcasters.org
State Film Commission: filmwisconsin.org
Media Markets—Milwaukee (33), Green Bay (69), Madison (85), La Crosse (123), Wausau (134)

Media Programs

University	City	Department / School
Marquette University	Milwaukee	J. William & Mary Diederich College of Communication
University of Wisconsin, Eau Claire	Eau Claire	Communication and Journalism
University of Wisconsin, La Crosse	La Crosse	Communication Studies
University of Wisconsin, Madison	Madison	Journalism & Mass Communication
University of Wisconsin, Milwaukee	Milwaukee	Journalism and Mass Communications
University of Wisconsin, Oshkosh	Oshkosh	Journalism
University of Wisconsin, Platteville	Platteville	Communication Technologies
University of Wisconsin, River Falls	River Falls	Journalism
University of Wisconsin, Stevens Point	Stevens Point	Communication
University of Wisconsin, Whitewater	Whitewater	Communication

Wyoming

State Broadcasting Association: wyomingbroadcasting.org
State Film Commission: wyomingfilm.org
Media Markets—Cheyenne (195), Casper (198)

Media Programs

University	City	Department / School
University of Wyoming	Laramie	Communication and Journalism

B Employment Websites

Most broadcast stations, corporate producers, newspapers, periodicals, and media specialists have their own websites. Those seeking employment with a specific employer should visit that employer's individual website. The following list of links is not meant to be all-inclusive, however, for those seeking employment or internships in the media, the websites listed here will provide a variety of opportunities.

www.2-pop.com
    The Digital Filmmaker's Resource Cite. It has a forum to discuss jobs, products, and other events of interest.

www.aaja.org
    Asian American Journalists Association. A list of job sources can be found under the Resources tab. AAJA also has multiple links to other items of interest, including news outlets, student programs, convention information, and industry news.

www.about.com
    About.com is one of the best websites, with links to many other media job sites. It also has numerous articles relating to job searches, such as preparing resumes and tapes. Click on Jobs/Careers, then click on Media/Arts.

www.afi.com
    In addition to information about the film industry, the American Film Institute's website lists a few job opportunities and workshops.

www.alliancecm.org
    The Alliance for Community Media's website discusses Public, Educational, and Governmental (PEG) access channels. It lists jobs, scholarships, and contact information for PEG channels.

www.americansportscastersonline.com
    The American Sportscasters Online website has a job bank that is frequently updated and offers listings free of charge. The listings are for television and radio sports positions.

www.ap.org/apjobs
    The Associated Press's website does not post specific jobs, but there is contact information for those interested in the AP's radio, print, TV, technology, online, sales, and administrative divisions.

www.askcbi.org
    The website for Collegiate Broadcasters, Inc., provides a wealth of information for students interested in broadcasting, including jobs, scholarships, and awards.

www.assignmenteditor.com
    Assignment Editor is an extensive site with multiple links for journalists. Once you are registered, there is a link to Media Jobs/Internships, which allows access to its employment database.

www.awrt.org
    The American Women in Radio and Television website has a CareerLine

link, but one must be a member to use it. The membership fee for students is $30.

www.b-roll.net

b-roll.net is a website dedicated to television photography. Its free job listings are for those who shoot and edit video. The site is frequently updated and is an excellent source of jobs for videographers.

www.beaweb.org

The Broadcast Education Association's website has a Job Openings link, which is updated several times a week. The positions listed are for those teaching broadcasting in higher education. The website also has an annual salary survey, so one can research how much money can be earned teaching mass media at the college level.

www.careerbuilder.com

Career Builder is an extensive site that allows employment searches in any field by keywords. One can specify a city, state, or category if desired.

www.careerpage.org

A free service of the National Alliance of State Broadcasters Associations, this website allows job searches by keyword. It also has links to NASBA website's divided by state associations for those with searches in specific locations.

www.cbscareers.com/main/index.aspx

This employment website for CBS also posts information for its corporate partners, including Viacom, King World, and UPN.

www.ccnma.org

The California Chicano News Media Association's website has job listings posted in print, television, advertising, public relations, technical, education, and other fields. Most positions are in California, but some are scattered in other states.

http://chronicle.com

This searchable site from the Chronicle of Higher Education is written for those teaching at colleges and universities. An extensive employment database allows search by keyword.

www.clearcareers.com

Clear Channel is the country's largest radio chain, and its website allows job searches by keyword, location, or job category.

www.cpb.org/jobline

The Corporation for Public Broadcasting's website is searchable for jobs and internships in public radio and television. Job categories, salary range, locations, and full-time/part-time status may be used as search variables.

www.cspan.org

C-SPAN's website offers a listing of employment opportunities and internships for its broadcast operations. Virtually all of the jobs are at its offices in Washington, DC.

www.current.org

Current Newspaper covers public television and radio throughout the country, thus this website has online elements of that newspaper. The jobs bank lists positions at public television and radio stations nationwide.

www.dga.org

The Directors Guild of America's website does not offer a job bank, but it has a DGA Members Directory so one can locate Guild members.

www.editorandpublisher.com

This website for Editor & Publisher contains much information about the newspaper industry, as well as a list of job postings, primarily for those in print media.

www.entertainmentcareers.net

This website lists media jobs and internships in the United States and other countries. Jobs range from news producers to costume designers to drivers—literally, the entire gamut of media professionals and support staff.

www.filmstaff.com

An extensive listing of television and film jobs, but it requires a subscription ranging from $4.95 per week to $99 per year.

www.foxcareers.com

This website offers job and internship information for the Fox Network and its corporate partners, including FX, National Geographic Channel, and Twentieth Century Fox Studios.

www.higheredjobs.com

This website, dedicated to those seeking employment in collegiate teaching, allows searches by keyword, location, and various categories.

www.hisair.net

A complete list of job opportunities at Christian radio stations is available, as is an extensive list of Christian radio station websites worldwide.

www.insideradio.com

Radio formats, stations, and directories are listed here, as well as a job listings database.

www.ire.org

The Investigative Reporters and Editors, Inc.'s website is for investigative journalists in both broadcast and print media. A Job Center database is available and does not required IRE membership.

www.journalismjobs.com

Journalism.Jobs.com's website is an extensive, searchable database of jobs and internships in television, radio, print, and online media, as well as public relations and related fields. Resumes can be posted for potential employers.

www.jpc.com

The Jefferson-Pilot Communications Company's website lists job opportunities for its 18 radio stations, 3 television stations, and Jefferson-Pilot Sports.

www.mandy.com

Mandy.com is a website that specializes in international film and television production crew resources both in the United States and worldwide. Production jobs are posted by continent and job position.

www.maslowmedia.com

The Maslow Media Group's website offers production staffing and services, camera crews, payroll, and government and media services.

www.mediabistro.com

The mediabistro.com website, owned by Jupitermedia Corporation, covers media news and events, but has job listings that span print and broadcast media.

www.medialine.com

Medialine's website allows job searches and resume postings, but members must subscribe to the service. Rates range from a 5-day listing for $9.95 to a 91-day access subscription for $67.50.

www.mediastaffingnetwork.com

Media Staffing Network's website has jobs and internships listed in advertising, broadcast, cable, direct response, new media, outdoor, and print industries.

www.nab.org

The National Association of Broadcasters' website has a career center for broadcast media jobs, as well as industry news, directories, and a schedule of upcoming events.

www.nabj.org

The National Association of Black Journalists' website has a database of jobs, but requires a membership fee of $25 for students or $80 for full members.

www.nahj.org

The National Association of Hispanic Journalists' website lists jobs in print, broadcast, communications, radio, new media, and academic categories, but it is only available to paying members. Annual student membership is $25, and a regular annual membership is $75.

www.narip.com

The National Association of Recording Industry Professionals' website lists jobs in the music & recording industries.

www.natpe.org

The National Association of Television Program Executives' website has a Career Center that allows both job searches and posting resumes.

www.nbcuni.com/About_NBC_Universal/Careers/

The website for NBC Television and corporate partner Universal Film provides information about careers, plus links to allied channels.

www.nbs-aerho.org

The National Broadcasting Society's website has many links to media organizations and to state broadcasting/cable websites.

www.npr.org/about/jobs

National Public Radio's website lists full-time and part-time jobs, as well as internships [see also NextGen: National Public Radio (Next Generation Radio) www.npr.org/about/nextgen/content/]

www.nrb.org

The National Association of Religious Broadcasters' website lists positions for Christian communicators through its Career Search/Classifieds link.

www.pbs.org/aboutpbs/jobsdatabase

The Public Broadcasting System's website lists its available jobs in public television. The listing consists of positions at its headquarters in Alexandria, Virginia.

www.productionhub.com

The Production Hub's website has an extensive directory of crew members for film and media projects. Although the site does not list available jobs, it does serve as a source of contact information in the industry.

www.radioannouncers.freehosting.net

This website is dedicated to radio announcers. There is a one-time membership fee of $10, which allows a user to post a resume and search for jobs. Members are also given free access to read the founder's book, *How to Get a Job in Radio.*

www.RadioLinks.net/Jobs

The Radio Links' website does not have a specific list of jobs, but it contains links to state broadcasting associations' job banks and other databases.

www.radio-online.com

RADIO ONLINE's website has information covering all of the latest in radio news, promotion, and personalities. A $10 monthly subscription allows access to its radio employment database.

www.rapmag.com

An online Radio and Production Magazine, this website has a limited list of jobs under its Classified section.

www.radioandrecords.com

With news and information about the latest in radio, this website has a limited list of jobs under its Resources section.

www.rtnda.org

The Radio-Television News Directors Association and Foundation website has information on awards, grants, news releases, and associated topics. It has a searchable job database under the Careers tab.

www.spj.org

The website for the Society of Professional Journalists has a wealth of information, but a membership is required to access its Career Center. Membership costs $72 per year, although students and recent college graduates can join for $36 annually.

www.timewarner.com/corp/careers/index.html

This website for Time Warner offers employment information for Warner Brothers, Turner Broadcasting, HBO, New Line Cinema, and other corporate partners.

http://tvandradiojobs.com

A searchable database of television, radio, music, and film positions.

www.tvjobs.com

A very thorough site with a wealth of information, including links to internships and a master station index. The Job Bank requires membership which ranges from one week for $9.95 to one year for $39.95.

www.tvspy.com

The website for TVSpy has news about the television news industry, as well as a job bank. A gold membership, which costs $29.85 for three months or $71.40 per year, is required to post resumes.

www.voa.gov/vacancies/personnel.html

The Voice of America employment website also has links to other governmental bureaus with an international reach, such as TV Marti and the International Broadcasting Bureau. Many of the jobs are in overseas positions.

http://wict.broadbandcareers.com

This is the Career Center page for Women in Cable and Telecommunications. The searchable database offers behind-the-scenes, technical positions.

www.womensportsjobs.com

News and information for women interested in sports, Women Sport Jobs' site has a subscription service for women's jobs in sports businesses, including broadcasting. Memberships to the job site are $24.99 for one month, although there are discounts for three-month or annual memberships.

C Media Organizations in the United States

There are more than 3,200 institutions of higher education functioning in the United States, with about 12,000 publications being produced by their students. The print publications include newspapers, yearbooks, literary and general magazines, newsletters, scholarly journals, booklets, pamphlets, humor magazines, underground publications, and even little broadsides. For electronic media, there is no shortage of student-operated television and radio stations. Each of these outlets provides the opportunity for hands-on training to supplement collegiate instruction.

Additionally, students should work with media organizations to learn more about their respective fields. The following list details some of the groups related to journalism, media, public relations, and the film industries. Some of these groups allow students to form chapters on individual campuses; interested students should contact these groups directly for registration information.

If a media organization does not provide for student chapters, the groups' websites offer valuable information on employment, conventions, contests, scholarships, and industry news. Additionally, virtually every film production house, newspaper, broadcaster, and media outlet has a website for those desiring information on a specific company.

AASFE: American Association of
   Sunday and Feature Editors
   www.aasfe.org/

ACES: American Copy Editors Society
   www.copydesk.org/

AJHA: American Journalism Historians
   Association
   http://ajhaonline.org/

ASJA: American Society of Journalists
   and Authors
   www.asja.org

ASNE: American Society of Newspaper
   Editors
   www.asne.org

AAJA: Asian American Journalists
   Association
   www.aaja.org

ACP: Associated Collegiate Press
   www.studentpress.org

APME: Associated Press Managing
   Editors
   www.apme.com

APSE: Associated Press Sports
   Editors
   http://apse.dallasnews.com/

AEJMC: Association for Education in
   Journalism and Mass Communication
   http://aejmc.org/

AOPE: Association of Opinion Page
   Editors
   www.psu.edu/dept/comm/aope/

AWC: Association for Women in
   Communications
   www.womcom.org

BEA: The Broadcast Education Association
www.beaweb.org

CAJ: The Canadian Association of Journalists
www.eagle.ca/caj/

CCNMA: California Chicano News Media Association
www.ccnma.org/

CBI: College Broadcasters, Inc.
www.askcbi.org/

CMA: College Media Advisors
www.collegemedia.org/

CNBAM: College Newspaper Business & Advertising Managers, Inc.
www.cnbam.org

CSPA: Columbia Scholastic Press Association
www.columbia.edu/cu/cspa/

CCJ: Committee for Concerned Journalists
www.concernedjournalists.org/

CPJ: Committee to Protect Journalists
www.cpj.org/

CCJA: Community College Journalism Association
www.ccjaonline.org/

The Freedom Forum
www.freedomforum.org/

Inland Press Association
www.inlandpress.org/

IDA: International Documentary Association
www.documentary.org

IPI: International Press Institute
www.freemedia.at/cms/ipi/

ISWNE: International Society of Weekly Newspaper Editors
www.mssu.edu/iswne/

IRE: Investigative Reporters and Editors
www.ire.org/

JAWS: Journalism and Women Symposium
www.jaws.org/

JEA: Journalism Education Association
www.jea.org

NABJ: National Association of Black Journalists
www.nabj.org/

NAB: National Association of Broadcasters
www.nab.org/

NAHJ: National Association of Hispanic Journalists
www.nahj.org/

NAMIC: National Association of Minorities in Communications
www.namic.com/

NCEW: National Conference of Editorial Writers
www.ncew.org/

NFPW: National Federation of Press Women
www.nfpw.org/

NFOIC: National Freedom of Information Coalition
http://reporters.net/

NLGJA: National Lesbian and Gay Journalists Association
www.nlgja.org/

NNA: National Newspaper Association
www.nna.org

NPC: National Press Club
http://npc.press.org/

NPPA: National Press Photographers Association
www.nppa.org/

NSPA: National Scholastic Press Association
www.studentpress.org/nspa

NSNC: National Society of Newspaper Columnists
www.columnists.com/

NAJA: Native American Journalists Association
www.naja.com/

NAA: Newspaper Association of America
www.naa.org/

TNG: The Newspaper Guild: Communications Workers of America
www.newsguild.org/

NextGen: National Public Radio (Next Generation Radio)
www.npr.org/about/nextgen/content/

ONA: Online News Association
www.onlinenewsassociation.org/

ONO: Organization of News Ombudsmen
www.newsombudsmen.org/

Poynter Institute for Media Studies
www.poynter.org/

PRNDI: Public Radio News Directors
www.prndi.org/

PRSSA: Public Relations Student Society of America
www.prssa.org

RTNDA: Radio and Television News Directors Association
www.rtnda.org/

RNA: Religion Newswriters Association
www.rna.org/

RCFP: Reporters Committee for Freedom of the Press
www.rcfp.org/

SBE: Society of Broadcast Engineers
www.sbe.org

SCJ: Society for Collegiate Journalists
www.scj.us

SEJ: Society of Environmental Journalists
www.sej.org

SND: Society for News Design
www.snd.org

SPJ: The Society of Professional Journalists
www.spj.org/

SNPA: Southern Newspaper Publishers Association
www.snpa.org/

SPLC: Student Press Law Center
www.splc.org

UFVA: University Film & Video Association
www.ufva.org

UNITY: Journalists of Color
www.unityjournalists.org/

YEA: Youth Editors Alliance
www.naa.org/foundation/yea/

D Media Festivals in the United States and Canada

A Student Guide

Media Festival Name	Website Address	Location
1. The $100 Film Festival	www.csif.org	Calgary, Canada
2. Action/Cut Short Film Festival	www.actioncut.com	Los Angeles, CA USA
3. AFI Fest	www.afi.com/onscreen/afifest	Los Angeles, CA USA
4. Anchorage Int'l Film Festival	www.anchoragefilmfestival.com	Anchorage, AK USA
5. Angelus Awards	www.angelus.org	Hollywood, CA USA
6. Ann Arbor Film Festival	www.aafilmfest.org	Ann Arbor, MI USA
7. Arizona Int'l Film Fest	www.azmac.org	Tucson, AZ USA
8. ARPA Foundation Film Festival (AFFMA)	www.affma.org	Hollywood, CA USA
9. The American Society of Cinematographers (ASC)—Charles B. Lang Heritage Award	www.theasc.com	Los Angeles, CA USA
10. Asheville Film Festival	www.ashevillefilmfestival.com	Asheville, NC USA
11. Ashland Independent Film Festival	www.ashlandfilm.org	Ashland, OR USA
12. Aspen Shortsfest	www.aspenfilm.org	Aspen, CO USA

(continued)

Media Festival Name	Website Address	Location
13. Athens (Ohio) Int'l Film Festival	www.athensfest.org	Athens, OH USA
14. Atlanta Film Festival	http://atlantafilmfestival.com/	Atlanta, GA USA
15. Attack of the 50 Foot Reels	www.flickerla.com/attack	Hollywood, CA USA
16. Austin Film Festival	www.austinfilmfestival.com	Austin, TX USA
17. Austin Gay and Lesbian Film Festival	www.agliff.org	Austin, TX USA
18. Avignon Film Festival/New York	www.avignonfilmfest.com	New York, NY USA
19. Banff Mountain Film Festival	www.banffcentre.ca/mountainculture	Banff, Canada
20. Beverly Hills Film Festival	www.beverlyhillsfilmfestival.com	Beverly Hills, CA USA
21. Big Muddy Film Festival	www.bigmuddyfilm.com	Carbondale, IL USA
22. Big Sky Documentary Film Festival	www.bigskyfilmfest.org	Missoula, MT USA
23. Boston Film Festival	www.bostonfilmfestival.org	Boston, MA USA
24. Boston Int'l Film Festival	www.bifilmfestival.com	Boston, MA USA
25. Boston Motion Picture Awards	www.bostonawards.com	Boston, MA USA
26. Boulder Int'l Film Festival	www.biff1.com	Boulder, CO USA
27. Brooklyn Int'l Film Festival	www.brooklynfilmfestival.org	New York, NY USA
28. Brooklyn Underground Film Festival	www.brooklynunderground.org	Brooklyn, NY USA
29. Carolina Film Festival	www.carolinafilmandvideofestival.org	UNCG in Greensboro, NC USA

(continued)

Media Festival Name	Website Address	Location
30. Chicago Int'l Documentary Festival	www.chicagodocfestival.org	Chicago, IL USA
31. Chicago Int'l Film Festival	www.chicagofilmfestival.org	Chicago, IL USA
32. Cine Golden Eagle Film and Video Competition	www.cine.org	Washington, DC USA
33. Cinequest	www.cinequest.org	San Jose, CA USA
34. Cleveland Film Festival	www.clevelandfilm.org	Cleveland, OH USA
35. College Television Awards (Student Emmys)	www.emmys.tv/foundation	Los Angeles, CA USA
36. Columbus Int'l Film and Video Festival	www.chrisawards.org	Columbus, OH USA
37. Coney Island Film Festival	www.coneyislandfilmfestival.com	Brooklyn, NY USA
38. Crossroads Film Festival	www.crossroadsfilmfest.com	Jackson, Mississippi USA
39. Cucalorus Film Festival	www.cucalorus.org	Wilmington, NC USA
40. Da Vinci Film & Video Festival	www.davinci-days.org	Corvallis, OR USA
41. Dance for the Camera	www.dance.utah.edu	Salt Lake City, UT USA
42. Dance on Camera Festival	www.dancefilmsassn.org	New York, NY USA
43. Dances with Films	www.danceswithfilms.com	Los Angeles, CA USA
44. Dawson City Int'l Film Festival	www.kiac.org	Dawson City, Yukon, Canada
45. DC Film Festival	www.filmfestdc.org	Washington, DC USA
46. DC Independent Film Festival	www.dciff.org	Washington, DC USA
47. deadCENTER Film Festival	www.deadcenterfilm.org	Oklahoma City, OK USA

(continued)

Media Festival Name	Website Address	Location
48. DGA Student Filmmaker Awards	www.dga.org	Los Angeles, CA USA
49. DOXA Documentary and Video Festival	www.doxafestival.ca	Vancouver, BC, Canada
50. Dragon Con Independent Short Film Festival	www.dragoncon.org	Atlanta, GA USA
51. Durango Film Festival	www.durangofilmfestival.com	Durango, CO USA
52. East Lansing Film Festival	www.elff.com	East Lansing, MI USA
53. Festival de Cinema des 3 Ameriques	www.fc3a.com	Montreal, Canada
54. Flicker	www.flickerla.com	Los Angeles, CA USA
55. Florida Film Festival	www.floridafilmfestival.com	Orlando, FL USA
56. Ft. Lauderdale Int'l Film Festival	www.fliff.com	Ft. Lauderdale, FL USA
57. Full Frame Documentary Film Festival	www.fullframefest.org	Durham, NC USA
58. Garden State Film Festival	www.gsff.org	Asbury, NJ USA
59. Gen Art Film Festival	ww.genart.org	New York, NY USA
60. George Lindsey UNA Festival	www.lindseyfilmfest.com	UNA in Florence, AL USA
61. H2O Hip Hop Odyssey Film Festival	www.h2oiff.org	Bronx, NY USA
62. Hamptons Film Festival	www.hamptonsfilmfest.org	Hamptons, NY USA
63. Hardacre Film Festival	www.hardacrefilmfestival.com	Tipton, IA USA
64. Heartland Film Festival	www.heartlandfilmfestival.org	Indianapolis, IN USA
65. High Falls Film Festival	www.highfallsfilmfestival.com	Rochester, NY USA

(continued)

Media Festival Name	Website Address	Location
66. Hot Docs	www.hotdocs.ca	Toronto, Canada
67. IDA / David L. Wolper Student Achievement Award	www.documentary.org	Los Angeles, CA USA
68. IFP Los Angeles Film Fest	www.lafilmfest.com	Los Angeles, CA USA
69. Image Out Rochester Gay & Lesbian Film Festival	www.imageout.org	Rochester, NY USA
70. Indianapolis Int'l Film Festival	www.indyfilmfest.org	Indianapolis, IN USA
71. Inside Out	www.insideout.on.ca	Toronto, Canada
72. Int'l Experimental Cinema Exposition	www.experimentalcinema.com	Colorado Springs, CO USA
73. Int'l Family Film Festival	www.iffilmfest.org	Universal City, CA USA
74. Int'l Film & Video Awards	www.newyorkfestivals.com	New York, NY USA
75. Int'l Student Film Festival-Hollywood	www.isffhollywood.org	Hollywood, CA USA
76. Int'l Wildlife Film Festival	www.wildlifefilms.org	Missoula, MT USA
77. Ivy Film Festival	www.ivyfilmfestival.com	Providence, RI USA
78. Jackson Hole Film Festival	www.jhff.org	Jackson Hole, WY USA
79. Jacksonville Film Festival	www.jacksonvillefilmfestival.com	Jacksonville, FL USA
80. Johns Hopkins Film Festival	www.jhu.edu/~jhufilm/fest	Baltimore, MD USA
81. Kansas City Filmmakers Jubilee	www.kcjubilee.org	Kansas City, MO USA
82. KODAK Filmschool Competition	www.kodak.com/go/filmschoolcompetition	

(continued)

Media Festival Name	Website Address	Location
83. LA Shorts Fest	www.lashortsfest.com	Hollywood, CA USA
84. Maine Int'l Film Festival	www.miff.org	Waterville, ME USA
85. Malibu Film Festival	www.malibufilmfestival.org	Malibu, CA USA
86. Manhattan Short Film Festival	www.msfilmfest.com	New York, NY USA
87. Maui Film Festival	www.mauifilmfestival.com	Maui, HI USA
88. Media City Int'l Festival of Experimental Film & Video Art Free	www.houseoftoast.ca/mediacity	Windsor, Canada
89. New York Film Festival	www.filmlinc.com	New York, NY USA
90. New York Int'l Children's Film Festival	www.gkids.com	New York, NY USA
91. New York Underground Film Festival	www.nyuff.com	New York, NY USA
92. Newport Beach Film Festival	www.newportbeachfilmfest.com	Newport Beach, CA USA
93. Newport Int'l Film Festival	www.newportfilmfestival.com	Newport, RI USA
94. NextFrame - UFVA's Touring Festival of Int'l Student Film & Video	www.temple.edu/nextframe	Philadelphia, PA USA
95. Outfest	www.outfest.org	Los Angeles, CA USA
96. Palm Springs Int'l Short Film Festival	www.psfilmfest.org	Palm Springs, CA USA
97. Pan-African Film Festival	www.paff.org	Los Angeles, CA USA
98. Philadelphia Film Festival	www.phillyfests.com	Philadelphia, PA USA
99. Phoenix Film Festival	www.phoenixfilmfestival.com	Phoenix, AZ USA

(continued)

Media Festival Name	Website Address	Location
100. Port Townsend Film Festival	www.ptfilmfest.com	Port Townsend, WA USA
101. Portland Int'l Film Festival	www.nwfilm.org/festivals	Portland, OR USA
102. Rhode Island Int'l Film Festival	www.film-festival.org	Providence, RI USA
103. River Run Film Festival	www.riverrunfilm.com	Winston-Salem, NC USA
104. Sacramento Film and Music Festival	www.sacfilm.com	Sacramento, CA USA
105. San Diego Film Festival	www.sdff.org	San Diego, CA USA
106. San Fernando Valley Int'l Film Festival	www.viffi.org	North Hollywood, CA USA
107. San Francisco Doc Fest	www.sfindie.com	San Francisco, CA USA
108. San Francisco Film Festival	www.sfiff.org	San Francisco, CA USA
109. San Francisco Indie Fest	www.sfindie.com	San Francisco, CA USA
110. San Francisco Jewish Film Festival	www.sfjff.org	San Francisco, CA USA
111. Santa Barbara Film Festival	www.sbfilmfestival.org	Santa Barbara, CA USA
112. Santa Cruz Film Festival	www.santacruzfilmfestival.com	Santa Cruz, CA USA
113. Santa Fe Film Festival	www.santafefilmfestival.com	Santa Fe, NM USA
114. Sarasota Film Festival	www.sarasotafilmfest.com	Sarasota, FL USA
115. Savannah Film Festival	www.scad.edu/filmfest	Savannah, GA USA
116. Seattle Film Festival	www.seattlefilm.com	Seattle, WA USA
117. Sedona Int'l Film Festival	www.sedonafilmfestival.com	Sedona, AZ USA

(continued)

Media Festival Name	Website Address	Location
118. Shockerfest	www.shockerfest.com	Modesto, CA USA
119. SIGGRAPH	www.siggraph.org	Los Angeles, CA USA
120. Silver Docs: AFI Documentary Film Festival	www.silverdocs.com	Silver Springs, MD USA
121. Slamdance	www.slamdance.com	Park City, UT USA
122. Smogdance	www.smogdance.com	Claremont, CA USA
123. Sonoma Film Festival	www.cinemaepicuria.org	Sonoma, CA USA
124. Spokane GLBT Film Fest	www.spokanefilmfest.org	Spokane, WA USA
125. Sundance Film Festival	www.sundance.org	Park City, UT USA
126. SXSW Film Conference and Festival	www.sxsw.com/film	Austin, TX USA
127. Syracuse Film & Video Festival	www.syrfilmfest.com	Syracuse, NY USA
128. Tambakos Student Video Competition	www.merrimack.edu/tambakos	North Andover, MA USA
129. Telluride Film Festival	www.telluridefilmfestival.com	Telluride, CO USA
130. Temecula Valley Int'l Film and Music Festival	www.tviff.com	Temecula, CA USA
131. Thunderbird Int'l Film Festival	www.thunderbirdfilmfestival.suu.edu	Cedar City, UT USA
132. Tiburon Film Festival	www.tiburonfilmfestival.com	Tiburon, CA USA
133. Trenton Film Festival	www.trentonfilmfestival.org	Trenton, NJ USA
134. Tribeca Film Festival	www.tribecafilmfestival.org	New York, NY USA
135. UberCon Gaming Convention's Independent Film Festival	www.ubercon.com	Meadowlands, NJ USA

(continued)

Media Festival Name	Website Address	Location
136. Urbanworld	www.urbanworld.com	New York, NY USA
137. USA Film Festival	www.usafilmfestival.com	Dallas, TX USA
138. Vail Film Festival	www.vailfilmfestival.org	Vail, CO USA
139. Vancouver Int'l Film Festival	www.viff.org	Vancouver, Canada
140. VC Film Fest	www.vconline.org	Los Angeles, CA USA
141. Vermont Int'l Film Festival	www.vtiff.org	Burlington, VT USA
142. Victoria Independent Film & Video Festival	www.vifvf.com	Victoria, BC, Canada
143. VisionFest	www.domanivision.org	New York, NY USA
144. Waterfront Film Festival for Children and Youth	www.waterfrontfilm.org	Saugatuck, MI USA
145. Westchester County Film Festival	www.westchestergov.com/filmoffice	White Plains, NY USA
146. Whistler Film Festival	www.whistlerfilmfestival.com	Whistler, Canada
147. Wild and Scenic Environmental Film Festival	www.syrcl.org/filmfest	Nevada City, CA USA
148. Wine Country Film Festival	www.winecountryfilmfest.com	Sonoma & Napa, CA USA
149. Women of Color Film Festival	www.bampfa.berkeley.edu/pfa_programs	Berkeley, CA USA
150. Worldfest Houston	www.worldfest.org	Houston, TX USA
151. Worldwide Short Film Festival	www.worldwideshortfilmfest.com	Toronto, Canada

DISCARD